Shout

an anthology of
Resistance
Poetry and Short Fiction

edited by

Benjamin Gorman
and Zack Dye

Published in the United States by
Not a Pipe Publishing, Independence, Oregon.
www.NotAPipePublishing.com

Paperback Edition

ISBN-13: 978-1-948120-45-6

Cover model: Sang Kromah. Cover design: Benjamin Gorman.

This is a work of fiction. Names, characters, places, and incidents either are products
of the writer's imagination or are used fictitiously.

Table of Contents

Introduction

When we conceived of this anthology, we wanted to give writers and poets an opportunity to stand up and be counted among the ranks of the brave activists, journalists, politicians, and other leaders who have risked their reputations and more to say, "This is wrong. This growing fascism in America is evil, and I will not sit silently and let it metastasize in the heart of my country." The pieces you'll read here are courageous in so many ways; these artists are bringing their full talents to bear to do their part to fight back. We're incredibly proud of the collection you're about to read. And the fact that you are engaging in this way, especially when the material is the most difficult to stomach, will hopefully inspire you to stand up and be counted as well.

A shocking number of the submissions we received were fantasies about Donald Trump's assassination. None of those are included. For the record, we do not believe Donald Trump should be killed, and we don't believe any of the writers fantasizing about that do, either. The man belongs in a cell. The fact that so many people, when asked to contribute to an anthology of resistance literature, crafted and sent stories where the President gets his comeuppance speaks to a boiling frustration at justice denied.

Donald Trump is an indictment of our criminal justice system, and, more profoundly, of the moral rot which undermines our desire for a just society. He is directly or indirectly responsible for more death, rape, kidnapping, theft, and a myriad of lesser crimes than anyone currently serving time in the prisons of the country that incarcerates a higher percentage of its population than any nation on Earth. Yet he walks free. He wasn't raised to properly value decency or kindness. He failed to make more out of what was given to him than someone with no business training could have made through passive investing; the fortune he did amass is the product of borrowing, unethical self-dealing, outright theft, and a carefully polished illusion that he's successful. It's a scam. His interpersonal behavior is abominable and frequently criminal. And yet, in spite of all of this, Donald Trump is not the problem. The man is a pustule. Criminal proceedings against him are entirely appropriate. But while it might relieve a painful pressure and might be a necessary part of preventing the further spread of an infection, lancing a boil does not treat the root cause of an illness. The problem is that too many of our fellow Americans are passively enabling or actively encouraging corruption, kidnapping, and mass murder out of political expediency, ginned-up partisan fear, and activated bigotry.

The United States is a very successful country by

many measures. Our military might and our wealth are currently unrivaled. Our standard of living, while declining for too much of our population, still allows some of the poorest among us to enjoy health and luxury the Pharaohs of Egypt would have envied. But this country was built on a foundation of injustice, built on stolen land by stolen people. It has always been ruled by those who, even when forced to expand representation, wanted to do so in a way that made sure they never had to give any of the proceeds of theft away. If we aren't making a concerted effort to address those fundamental injustices, we are not patriots who love any higher American value, just nationalists who value flexing our country's muscles.

Americans also now live in an era where facts have been shoved to the side. President Trump has been impeached based on clear and indisputable evidence, yet we argue about the veracity of facts. This creates a dystopian environment where we are unable to use the truth to adjudicate our problems. These are the conditions in banana republics and Orwellian fiction. The authors and poets in this anthology may not be able to change what Americans want to hear, but at least we can speak to the unreal nature of our misunderstandings. Within these pages, we remove facts and speak to deeper truths through worlds that are fantastically unreal; here we can combat the deceptive narratives of our politicians with our own honest fiction to warn about a future where we discard truth for injustice and greed.

Speaking out against injustice is difficult. For many of us, we feel like we're shouting into the void, potentially facing the social consequences of the disapproval of friends and family without the reward of knowing our statements make a tangible difference. Without that one-to-one, it can be difficult to feel motivated. Also, who wants to share the pain of those who are harmed? Who wants to carry around anger at those who cause that harm? For writers, we could justify silence in the face of injustice in so many ways:

"I'm a nobody. No one will read what I write. Who will care?"

"This isn't my particular brand. I'm not a political writer. I may diminish my audience."

"I'm not a journalist. What difference will my art make?"

"Can't I just make sure I'm being a good person, raise my kids in the right way, cross my fingers, and hope this whole thing will blow over?"

The writers in this anthology have made a different choice. They have decided to stand up and be counted. None of them can know exactly what consequences they will face. An angry relative? Trolls on twitter? Reduced sales of their next book? A stint in a Trump concentration camp? A firing squad? The latter sound absurd and paranoid, right?

In October of 2018, at a rally in Texas, the President of our country declared himself to be a "nationalist." This is the term fascist dictators use to describe themselves. If you aren't freaking out, we have a question for you: How many people will have to die before you will feel regret at not having acted sooner?

Please remember, there are lots of ways to kill a person without ever pulling a trigger.

- You could take healthcare from a sick person.
- You could take retirement income from an old person.
- You could pollute the air or water and poison a person.
- You could give weapons to someone who will kill thousands of people in Yemen or Syria.
- You could protect someone who is killing journalists in Turkey or the UK or Malaysia.
- You could lock up someone's children so someone else is too scared to come to your country and remains in deadly peril in their own.
- You could legally erase a group of people so their deaths won't be noticed.
- You could vilify a group of people so much that others fear them and kill them on sight.
- You could agitate for a nuclear arms race which could lead to the worst war in history.
- You could accelerate humanity's efforts to make our only home planet uninhabitable.

There are lots of ways to kill someone.

And before you point this out: Yes, Democratic politicians have, in their history, committed variations on some of these. But "what-about-isms" aren't justifications, and false equivalences are false.

Republican politicians are doing them ALL. Right now. They are working on accomplishing this whole list. They aren't even hiding it.

Now, your local Republican politicians will say, "Aw, shucks. I don't agree with Donald Trump on everything." Mostly, they wish he tweeted less. But every single one has signed on to further this agenda. We challenge you to find a single Republican who has spoken out against all the items on this list.

And blaming Republican politicians isn't enough. This is our country. "We the People." Citizens of every other country will look at us and say, "You are an American. What did you do? Did you vote them out? When you couldn't do that, did you speak out? Or did you say, 'I cast a ballot. After that, my hands were clean. Not my circus, not my monkeys. All those deaths: Not my problem.'"

It is your problem. If being an American is part of your identity, then every single thing the country does collectively is partly on you. That's the awesome and overwhelming responsibility of democracy: It associates all of us with things we disagree with. We often hold our noses and vote for the lesser of two evils. We are all morally compromised. It sucks.

But we are responsible adults, and we're now living in a country with an avowed nationalist as a President, and with a party controlling all three branches of government which is willing to sacrifice the lives of our allies, our neighbors, and our own citizens. None of us have any excuse for inaction. It's already past time to shout, "This is not right!"

Activist Charlotte Clymer wrote, "'Civility' has become a codeword for being asked to set yourself on fire to keep others warm." Yes, it will be uncomfortable to tell someone that the people they are supporting have a murderous agenda. You may be told to be more "civil." You may be cut off from friends and even disowned by some family. We have been. It hurts. But our President is an avowed nationalist. Fact beyond dispute. And after he is gone, the people who supported him will still expect to hold leadership positions and further the same agenda. Standing up to Trump is just the first step. Confronting the fascist agenda must be our goal. How many people have to die for that nationalist agenda to become more troubling than the discomfort of speaking out? How many unnecessary deaths can you live with? Put a number on it. Then carry that number around. And when we exceed that number, wonder why you didn't shout sooner.

-Benjamin Gorman and Zack Dye

The Triumph of Small Things

by Rosanne Parry

(Winter Solstice 2012,
one week after the Newtown school massacre)

Who are we to hope?
When darkness is everywhere so deep and so cold,
When the dinosaurs of evil seem so impossibly large and
    so permanent.
The very first archaeopteryx must have felt utterly alone,
A feathered thing in a world of armor and scales.
And yet who sings now in the bleak rain of a leafless
    forest?

Who are we to hope?
After 340 years of servitude and degradation in the state
    of Louisiana,
A little girl in a white dress went to school.
A black girl, age six, all forty-five pounds of her
Walked to school between four US Marshals,

Through throngs of her classmates' mothers.
One carried a child-sized coffin with a doll inside, a black
doll in a white dress.
And yet she walked. Chin up. Eye on the prize.

The unseen picture is just as potent.
The hand that laundered and starched and pressed that
dress,
That smoothed and twined those pigtails,
And sent her Ruby out into the dark,
Every day of that first grade year.

A dose of polio vaccine is four milliliters.
It weighs as much as the feather of a crow,
And it brought to its knees,
The disease that killed or crippled 57,000 children in a
year

When lost in the woods who survives
The thirty-five year old man or the four year old child?
It's a trick question.
The grown man does not believe he is lost.
Is sure if he climbs the next ridge, and the one after that
He will see his way home
And so presses on, along the path of the dinosaurs,
In spite of the rain and the dry clothes in his pack.

The child's strength is play.
Walking downhill is more fun.
Singing is less lonely.

Resting when she is tired isn't even a question.
And so the very next morning the child walks
Downhill
Singing
Into the arms of her family.

In the land of Judah in the face of oppression
When hope was thin on the ground,
The Jews found a hammer well-suited to the work at
    hand.
They spoke to their god and stood their ground.
They lit their lamps
 And lived.
It was not their first encounter with extermination.
It would not be their last.
Yet come what may, one century after another,
God's chosen light their candles and stand together
Eight candles
In the window
Against the dark.

And the winter wren, all one third of an ounce of him,
In the bare twigs of the forest,
Sings.

Growth

by Janet Burroway

(First published in the New Virginia Quarterly, Winter 1990)

The drains were already sealed when they moved in. Everything else seemed to work – electricity, internet, video screens, heat, the gas hob, plenty of water. The local shops delivered, not just food but clothes and toys, building supplies, appliances, gadgetry of all kinds; so it looked like a terrific neighborhood.

Of course they were lucky to get it. It was Georgian concrete, quite pretty, fenced back and sides, with a low hedge in front. The thing about the drains – well, some areas went before others, it was hard to predict where would be next, you took potluck; and really it was such old news that you couldn't work up any outrage over it.

They were a common type of suburban family, four-and-a-dog, Nancy and Peter, Daniel who was seven, and Ariella nine. *Ariella* as a name was their one flight of romance. Nancy had loved it ever since she was a little girl and saw a movie in which that was the heroine's name. The dog, Terry, was a terrier (the name was Ariella's choice; perhaps she did not like the extravagance of her own). Anyway, the house gave them a room apiece (arranged three for sleeping and one for Pete's computer set-up), two baths, a smallish parlor and a fair-sized kitchen, a quite pleasant dining room with a view out over the back porch to the grass of the yard.

The tub was plugged. The toilet had been removed altogether so Pete, who was handy, constructed a dressing table to hide the cement mess in the floor. Nancy set her sewing machine up in their bedroom and made a skirt for it out of peach and lemon seersucker plaid sent up from Whittaker's in town. It turned out really pretty.

Of course, the first thing that had to be resolved was sewage. The backyard was about twenty-five by forty (two old elms and a border of alyssum, in bloom when they arrived). Pete figured he could allow ten feet at the back for elm roots, divide the rest into nine squares of eight-by-ten each, and rotate the outhouse in an S pattern from the upper right hand corner to the lower left, digging a new pit every four months. This would take three years altogether, and by the time the last plot was offensive the first one would be sweetened again. There was the problem that in the third year, for the whole year, the privy would be in the section of the yard nearest the house where the dining room overlooked it. But it couldn't be helped.

So that was settled. Nancy was determined that they

were going to make a routine of their daily baths and not lower their standards of cleanliness. The children moaned and carried on – but she was a sensible, no-nonsense sort of mother and had let them cry in their cribs until they learned how to sleep through the night. So this time she steeled herself for the same long-haul of discipline, ignored their protests, stood her ground. They ran the water into the bath, bathed, then bailed, each one of them helping to fill the bucket for the others; Pete did most of the carrying out to the outhouse. It was part of the theory that this would help to wash the sewage down, but in fact after a few weeks it became clear that four tubs a day was more water than the ground could handle. It started to seep out around the base of the plank hut (funny how we retain certain images; the outhouse looked exactly like the ones Pete had known as a boy at camp). The air inside was wetter than it should have been, rank. The ground of half the backyard was just a little soggy. Nancy tried pouring more of the water on the alyssum, and into the much smaller plot – strip, really – of grass in front. But the ground was over-damp everywhere, so they had a family conference and decided that daily baths were, perhaps, a luxury that they had to forgo. It would be wise, even public-spirited, to do without them. It was decided that the children would bathe one day, Pete the next, Nancy the next. Non-bath days, they learned how to sponge-bathe, and later to wash off with just as much water on the cloth as would evaporate, so there was none to throw away at all.

You can't take it in all at once, not being able to get

rid of things. You can't foresee how it will thwart you. Nancy was reminded of a time when Danny was a forty-pound toddler and she had broken a tiny little bone in her wrist. The bone was minute – she forgot now what it was called – like a sliver of a fish bone, but it turned her life around. She had been able to lift Danny by her forearms, but she couldn't change a diaper, untwist a babyfood cap, slice vegetables, button his sweater. They had sat together in fret and squalor while she tried to calm him by rocking and singing to him. He was thoroughly spoiled before her wrist was healed.

Housekeeping now reminded her of that. She had to be inventive. She would sweep as much as she could into a dustpan and from that into a paper bag; or she could vacuum and throw the vacuum bags down the outhouse hole. But these threatened to fill the pit too fast, and after a while they decided to burn the bags in a pile in the backyard. Cleaning rags she rinsed over and over again in the same sludge, and then at the end of the day rinsed in a little clean water. When the rags got too filthy, Pete burned them in the backyard with the bags. The dust and fluff made a thick smoke, and from time to time (hard to predict) it would settle on the windows as grime, or on the sills as a fine dust.

Nancy went ahead and operated the washing machine for the heavier clothes. She ordered a surgical syringe from Reeves Supplies, and after each load, once for the washing cycle and twice for rinsing, she would suck on the tube until her mouth filled, then put it in a bucket to siphon the water off. The spin cycle couldn't be used of course, so the clothes were heavy with wet. Peter would help her carry them to the back, wring them, and spread them out on the fence.

They had a problem with Terry. You can't ask a dog to understand such notions as "turning the tide" or "maintenance model" or "sins of the father," the phrases that politicians love to use. So Terry resented the move, and he tended to express this anger by peeing in the corners or leaving a mushy turd on the carpet in Ariella's room. It had Nancy in tears more than once. It took so much water to wash out dog filth, and getting the rags clean wasn't really possible, so she ended up burning them as well. Also Terry had fleas, and both Nancy and Ariella got huge welts around their ankles from the bites.

Anything they wanted could be ordered from the shops, and catalogs and parcel service still arrived every day. You could hardly blame them for wanting the variety and freshness in their lives that new things bring; so that the children had toys and the grown-ups had reading matter – staring at screens got so old – and all of them had new clothes from time to time. But of course this acquiring meant that eventually there had to be discards; so some days Peter found himself burning cloth. The synthetics gave off a chemical odor but the wool was worse, a smoky sweetness that made you think of crematoria. And afternoons when they had done the burning they all had itchy eyes; Ariella's nose ran.

Also, some foodstuffs came in tins, and quite a proportion of the children's toys. Pete had to give up one corner of the garden, which meant one of his nine privy plots, to metal trash. They tried burning the plastic (food packaging and toys again), but when they did, the air hung with an acrid almost oily stench that none of them could breathe, so Pete stacked the plastic too.

One day he got up very early, filled two pillow slips with this stuff and with some old clothes, rags stiff with soil, and went out to find some place to dump it. But he was back in a few hours, disoriented from the attempt, and carrying the pillow cases. He said the ring road was dangerous to maneuver for the debris already there, and that nobody was let onto it without the right vehicles and safety equipment. Later that same week, they woke up to find that somebody had dumped four plastic sacks of garbage over the front hedge onto their grass strip, and Ariella (who had a tendency to piety in any case) said it served Daddy right! Pete said fine, she could do without anything new for the rest of the month. And he meant it; he was as disciplined a parent as Nancy.

Twice more the next week they woke to find bags or boxes pushed over the low front hedge into their yard. Pete spent a whole day sorting it, burning some, dumping the worst down the privy hole. Nancy said he should post the land, put up a sign. But he made a wry *big-deal* face at this. He proposed to keep watch. He stayed up every night for a week before he gave in and ordered stout pine from the lumberyard to complete the quadrangle of fence around them. Twice he had fallen asleep, and once a skin-and-bones cat had wandered in. At least Pete was skilled enough to dig the posts in between the hedge and the sidewalk; so they still had their privet to look at out the front windows.

Ariella sulked a little, about the ban on new amusements. She played a lot with Terry, rather ostentatiously, more than Terry seemed to enjoy. Pete and Nancy didn't in fact know if Terry's increased accidents indoors were a result of simple fatigue or if he were protesting being used in a family squabble. Pete, at any rate, suggested this latter anthropomorphic analysis. Nancy began to worry that Terry was sick, even infectious. The turds got softer and greener, she thought – and there was no denying that the fleas got worse. They tried to ignore it for longer than they should have, with the consequence that they had a full-scale infestation. They ordered a supply of fleas spray and bombs, soaked the carpets, set off the foggers, and then stayed outdoors for a couple of hours while the insecticides did their work. And they did seem to work, although the scent was oppressive, almost a feel in the air, which seemed to hang around and hang around.

Pete and Nancy decided that Terry would have to live in the backyard. This, of course, was a source of protest and bitter blame from both the children. But as soon as Terry started to live outdoors, he did what dogs do, rolled on the ground, showing a preference for where the damp seeped around the privy, and soon Ariella would not go near him, let alone have him in her room.

Now Danny got some sort of stomach bug, and Nancy began to worry about the water supply, which she thought smelled of sewage taint though of course it would be hard to tell. Somewhat over Pete's protest (he thought she was too quick to panic), she decided to boil and then strain the water. Pete reasoned that anything really lethal would go though cloth, but Nancy reasoned that the cloth could be used for cleaning afterward anyway, and at least she would know she was doing what she could. So Pete humored her, ordered a huge galvanized drum and a sheet of tin big enough to make a funnel for it, and they lined this with a quarter of a two-hundred-count percale sheet at a time, pure cotton. Nancy would keep water on the boil all day, pour each panful in the funnel, draw it from a spigot Pete rigged toward the bottom of the drum. In the second week of this, it came to Pete that the cotton sheets, which they ordered by the half dozen from the catalog, were impregnated with some no-iron chemical; so it was about even odds whether they were filtering more foreign matter into the water than out of it. But he did not say this to Nancy. He did not know an alternative to make her feel better. There was no point washing the sheets first – the washing machine used water from the tap; so they would be washing in the same elements or ingredients they were trying to filter out. He let it be. Nancy continued to boil and strain.

Terry, abandoned in the backyard, became scruffy and, at first, whiny, then truly bad-tempered. The day that he bit Danny on his way to the outhouse – a really nasty three-quarter inch tear in his calf—Pete and Nancy had a conference after the children had gone to bed. Each of them knew before they began what the other was thinking, and mostly, instead of talking, they held hands.

They held all four hands. It was one of the tenderest times they had experienced together since they moved in. They only thing they actually discussed was what to do with the body. Pete favored the outhouse because burial would mean the loss of another of the nine projected plots. But Nancy worried about Terry's being thrown down the current hole, not out of sentimentality but out of a fear that the children would somehow know he was there. They compromised that way: Peter would dispose of the dog down the privy but then bury him there, digging the third outhouse a month in advance of the plan. Nancy gave him a piece of polyester clothesline for a garotte, and Pete went out to take care of it. It took him all night. The children next morning were excited at the relative freshness of their new "bathroom" but made no mention of Terry's departure.

After that, Pete thought Nancy went a little nuts on hygiene. She had adjusted, trooper-like, to the one-bath-in three-days at the beginning, but now she got obsessive about floors and counter tops. She would scrub things down, rinse her sponge or rag, scrub them down again, rinse again, until the water was no cleaner than the thing she was washing and the exercise became pointless in the extreme. She noticed, and pointed out to them so they all began in spite of themselves to notice, how fetid is the smell of rotting vegetable matter. Worse than shit, she said – and it was worse. The privy stank worst of all when they had thrown out leftover cooked green beans or carrots, or still worse, asparagus or artichokes. Now there were shrill fights about finishing-everything-on-your-plate. Nancy pulled this even on Pete, and they fought about it after the children were asleep. Exotic foods were no longer worth the trouble. Nancy cooked less, and they ate healthy crisp salads, though she worried about whether these could be adequately rinsed.

In this period Nancy began to read *Pinocchio* to Danny, one of the loved books of her own childhood, and was pleased that Ariella, pretending indifference, would leave her video screen and perch on a chair at the edge of the room as if by accident, in transit. There was a scene in the story that Nancy brought back to the bedroom to read to Pete as well, in which Pinocchio demands that his pears be peeled and cored. He eats the flesh. Then still hungry, he goes back and eats the rest. Geppetto draws the thrifty moral, that if one is hungry enough, the palate loses its sophistication. But on this moral, Nancy mused. She was bemused. They were not poor, and food was plentiful. She would have to teach her children to eat all, however, all; because space to put the peel and core was precious.

Danny's dog bite did not heal well. She had sterilized it thoroughly and secured the skin together with one of the new "Medifine Stitch-Patch" kits, but where the flesh joined to itself it also puffed, and the red edges were an angry color oozing pus. Nancy was frantic. She forbade Danny the backyard. She ordered antibiotics and the latest salves. Pete tried arguing that it was bad for Danny to stay indoors all day fretting; the poor kid squeezed at his wound out of sheer boredom, he said. But for answer Nancy led Pete out back and took two or three deep breaths, inviting him by example to do the same. She stepped into the grass and pulled back her foot, directing him to look at how the water welled into it. She walked over and stood in front of the alyssum border, from which the blooms had faded in their proper season, but of which the stalks were now moldy in a way that suggested there would be no other season. The bark of the elms was scabrous. As they stood there mosquitoes and gnats found their necks, forearms. Pete said, "We must get some spray." Nancy did not reply. She went inside.

Soon after that, she missed her period and was feeling nauseated in the mornings, although she had used all the right precautions, even doubled up on them, pills and spermicide. The persistence of fecundity appalled her. In the second week the nausea became real sickness, and the odor of the outhouse so aggravated it that once she started vomiting there she hardly dared leave the hut. She had to tell Pete she was pregnant, then, and as she feared, his first reaction was that flash of temper that he used to show so often, the disappearance of which had been one compensation of this life. He apologized a few hours later and set to digging a new hole in the noxious garden on the fourth of his measured plots.

She didn't think about the future. Ariella screamed that she would not go into that new place, the sick smell revolting! So Nancy took Ariella into her confidence too, and tried to enlist both sympathy and complicity in the process of birth. Ariella remained only partly mollified, suspicious and wary, perhaps jealous, but whether of her mother's state or the fetus' status was not clear.

Danny sickened. He became flushed, thinner, sometimes complained of a chill. More and more of the time in front of his video screen he lay supine and didn't wander to the kitchen for a snack as he had used to do. His face took on a slightly adenoidal appearance, and his eyes were lusterless.

When Nancy's pregnancy had advanced about eight weeks, she began to develop a fear of the water supply. Her throat closed when she drank from the tap. One day the cool of the washcloth over her upper arms made the flesh crawl. She imagined that she was smearing microscopic filth onto the pallid surface of her skin. She ordered cases of Perrier and Evian and cut back on non-essential washing. She took her sponge bath in bottled water and made the children do the same. Pete refused. He put in extra hours at his computer, with the martyred air of a man whose wife wastes money. The backyard, which had been soggy, browned, and the hedge in front was sere.

Nancy sat by Danny's couch and read to him, rationed his extra washcloths full of Evian, and laved his face and neck, his skinny arms. Ironically the dog bite had healed now, the edges knit a little raggedly but without swelling or significant discoloration. Diagnoses had been stopped early in the self-sufficiency programs, but she didn't suffer from not knowing what he had. She suffered anomalously, a suffering without content, sitting by his side as he wasted.

She had to move him to his bed when he lost control of his bowels. She kept a rubber pad under his sheet and wiped it down with Evian. Neither would she wash his sheets in the poisoned water from the tap. They had plenty of Springmaid percale, and could order more from Simpson's whenever they liked. She just used as many sheets as she needed to, to keep Danny comfortable, and now without a demur Pete carried them to the backyard, where he burned them once a day. The smoke settled in a fine ash over the roof and on the sills. Nancy sat by Danny's bed and cooed him, leaned over her rounding belly and whispered nursery rhymes in his ear. He complained very little, was very quiet, and she did not think he was in pain. She thought about it very little. She just sang to him. And she thought about where on earth, where on earth, they were going to put him.

Disfiguring History

by Carolyn Adams

(November 8, 2016)

Unresolved,

That the constitution be laid bare,
without convention, stateless,
and in disagreement,
on the day the president is elected.

That from that time hence,
the time and place for
disorganized proceedings
shall not be fixed.

That no one shall assemble purposefully,
and no rolls created or completed.

That uncertified, unsigned,
unchosen votes are not counted,
and ballots removed from broken boxes.

That the republic shall diminish.

That the air is emptied of democracy.

Shout

by Benjamin Gorman

1

[1]Josue was walking home with his family after Easter mass. [2]As a deeply religious man, Easter was his favorite holiday, and because he took his second-greatest amount of joy from his family, watching his daughters skip ahead in their bright new spring dresses and listening to the sound of the little girls' laughter brightened his mood considerably. [3]But this Easter was tainted by some news that was upsetting Josue's wife, Maria. [4]At church, just before the service, she'd learned that her best friend and *comadre*, Veronica, godmother of his daughter Cecilia, had decided to make the journey.

[5]He spoke with his wife in a low voice to try to keep his words from floating to the ears of girls. [6]"The journey itself is very dangerous. And she will not get in when she arrives. There is The Wall, now."

[7]"If she stays, the gangs will certainly kill Little Emilio,"

Maria said. [8]"And you know Big Emilio has been drinking more. He beats her when he has been drinking. [9]She knows if she talks to Big Emilio about the gangs, he will become angry and probably beat them both. And if Little Emilio is killed, she thinks Big Emilio will probably beat her to death. [10]Maybe not right after, but when the house is lonelier and he is mourning, he will drink even more, and she will not have Little Emilio to protect her. [11]So if she stays, her son dies, and then she dies. [12]Her sister lives in *El Norte*, in Seattle, a city that is friendly to us. [13]If she can get there, her brother-in-law will let them live in his house, and her sister says she can work at the hotel with her. It would be a good life. [14]A good life or death? It is no choice."

[15]This was one of the longest speeches he'd ever heard from Maria. [16]She spoke it almost in a whisper to keep the news from the girls, her eyes aimed at the dirt trail in front of her to make it clear she was not contradicting him. [17]Yet there was a force in her words he had never heard. A steely anger. [18]Josue feared his wife's anger. When the girls misbehaved, she would chase them with *la chancla*, and he would say a prayer of thanks that he would never have to face that wrath. [19]He was as certain of this as he was of his knowledge that God made the world; Maria had been raised to defer to her husband in everything unless he violated a very short list of prohibitions, and since he knew he would never cheat on her, beat her, or sexually abuse their daughters, he could remain in her good graces for the rest of his happy life.

[20]Though she terrified him in her brief rages, Maria's smile always felt like his greatest victory. She smiled rarely, and that bright, toothy grin made him think of things he'd heard about in mass: choirs of angels and Jesus welcoming his chosen servants into his Father's house. [21]Most of the time Maria's face was placid. She was short, like him, with strong *india* features, a round face, flat nose, heavy eyebrows, and in this neutral gaze he would not notice her beauty. [22]He remembered it when she smiled. [23]But there was one expression that made her more beautiful than her smile. When she was sad, tears would pool in her eyes quickly, and her bottom lip would jut out just a bit, pressed down by her upper lip firmly holding her sadness in. [24]That was when she looked most beautiful to him, and also when he most desperately wanted to make her smile. [25]It seemed unfair to Josue that God would make Maria most beautiful when she was sad, but he did not question God's wisdom.

[26]As he contemplated this, he blinked in the mid-afternoon sun. [27]Unlike his wife, who had more Asiatic eyes to match her full cheeks, Josua had large eyes that tended to open too much, making him look permanently surprised by the world. [28]This was not the case; Josue's world was small, just their poor suburb of Guatemala City, and very little surprised him here. [29]The city was swallowing up their town, bringing the gangs and politics to the dirt streets between the cinderblock homes of the laborers who traveled into the city or out to the fields for work each day. [30]Now the gangs wanted their sons. Josue

was so glad he had only daughters, and that, at 27, he already looked too old to garner the interest of the local recruiters. [31]He was also too short, he thought. They wanted children who would grow up to be tall men, not young men who looked like old men ready to shrink down to the size of children. [32]He blinked at this thought. It challenged his masculinity only a little. [33]What did he care if the gangs did not respect him? [34]He had Maria and the girls. He had love and a house and a job. He did not want to think about the politics of the gangs and *El Norte* and The Wall.

[35]It was precisely at that moment, when he assured himself that he didn't need to be concerned with those things, that the old man appeared. [36]Josue blinked again. He hadn't noticed the man sitting on the stoop until the family was right next to him, and Josue usually had a good radar for men in his path, especially when he was walking with the girls. [37]But the man had been sitting so still. Maybe he'd only noticed the man when he'd lifted his head. [38]*Yes*, Josue thought, *surely he didn't appear. He had just been hiding. But how did I miss a beard so white?*

[39]The old man stood up slowly, not threatening, but he was much taller than Josue and walked with an imposing confidence as he approached them on the path that had become the road between the houses that now dotted the way from the church, and which would grow closer and closer and climb on top of one another until they became Guatemala City far off.

⁴⁰"*Señor*," the man said, "I must speak with you."

⁴¹Maria shot Josue a frightened glance, but he tried to reassure her. "You go on with the girls. I will not be long."

⁴²He turned back to the tall man with the long white beard. They didn't speak while Maria herded the girls ahead of her. ⁴³Once the men were alone, Josue said, "Are you with gangs or the *policia*? I do not get involved in politics."

⁴⁴"Neither," the tall man said. "I am the commander of the Army of the Lord. I have come."

⁴⁵The greatest miracle of the day, Josue would later reflect, was that he instantly knew this was the truth. ⁴⁶He fell down on the road and placed his forehead on the dirt, just as he'd heard about in the stories from the priests at church. ⁴⁷"What message does my Lord have for his servant?"

⁴⁸"Take off your sandals, for the place you are in is holy."

⁴⁹This, too, Josue understood. To Josue's right stood the home of the widow Consuela, a woman frequently accused of *brujeria* who, it was said, sold illegal potions to the young women of the village when they wanted abortions. To Josue's left: the town's one bar. It was hardly the location anyone would suspect of being a holy site. But Josue knew the presence of the angel sanctified the few meters around them. ⁵⁰Josue used his toes to pry

off his sandals because he couldn't reach them with his head on the ground, and he wasn't sure if he was supposed to get up.

[51]"Now, I will tell you what you must do," the angel said.

[52]Josue listened. He argued that he was too short, too quiet, and illiterate, and not a leader. [53]But the angel told him, "When you inform them that God will give them food and water on the journey, and that you are not a *coyote* who will charge them a fee, some will follow. [54]And once they see the bread falling from the sky and the water coming up from the stones, more will follow."

[55]"But what about Maria and my daughters?"

[56]"Leave them behind," the angel said.

[57]And that would be the hardest part. Josue would have to remind himself that this was a test of his faith with every step through the desert.

2

[1]The march took three months. [2]Just as the angel of the Lord had said, once the thin pancakes of unleavened bread began falling from the sky, and water started springing up from stones to provide for the migrants, news spread. [3]The caravan grew in size, and reporters swarmed the edges of the bedraggled army. [4]They numbered more than five hundred by the time they

crossed into Mexico, and the numbers continued to swell. [5]As they passed through the central plains of Mexico, helicopters from CNN swirled around the group almost constantly. [6]Some Americans, whether because they were of Central American or Mexican descent, or because they were Catholic and liked this humble man of God leading their people through the wilderness, or because they were liberals who wanted to give to the poor migrants out of a combination of compassion, guilt, and political spite, sent care packages with supplies ranging from bottled water, to tennis shoes, to shoeboxes with soap and small toys packed by children in far-away Sunday school classes, to t-shirts advertising the victory of the team that actually lost the last year's Superbowl. [7]Though they didn't really need the water, since they kept finding miraculous springs on their way, Josue told them to keep the bottles. [8]Some assumed this was because the caravan might pass through a stretch without water. Others thought he was trying to prevent litter. [9]But they did as they were told in this regard, since they had received so few instructions from the little man. It was a relief to know they had something else to do besides walk.

[10]The caravan did not march in a military formation. When the roads were thin, they strung out in a line that lasted for days. [11]When they hit the central plains of Mexico and left the roads, the group formed a loose amoeba of humanity, some extensions stretching ahead of the main group, others lagging far behind. [12]Because there always seemed to be reporters with cameras

walking backwards in front of him, Josue was never truly at the front of this caravan, but he was the amoeba's nucleus, his footfalls determining its direction. [13]He rarely spoke. Instead, he tried to listen. [14]The sound of five thousand people trudging and talking and breathing and laughing and whining and shouting formed one cohesive buzz behind him, and he carried this while also aiming his senses forward, trying to hear God's whispers in the wind across the hard-packed sand in front of him. [15]He was not used to so much noise, so much humanity. The caravan was larger than his town, more crowded than the largest suburbs of Guatemala City he'd ever dared to visit. He found all the sound oppressive. [16]At night he'd shiver at the songs of packs of coyotes sending eerie yips and high wails off to the foothills and back. [17]They didn't have packs of coyotes in Guatemala, and to him they sounded like a single monster stalking the group and herding them along God's way, reminding him that if he chose the wrong direction, this filthy beige Cerberus would take some of the women and children and rip them apart in its many howling mouths.

[18]The group had remarkable luck, though, if Luck is the god one prefers to credit. [19]In addition to the bread and water, they were spared the flash floods that sometimes raced across the desert after a deluge. At the hottest times of the day on the very hottest days, banks of clouds were sent to provide them shade. [20]There were no outbreaks of cholera or even the year's flu bug. [21]Only a few people rolled ankles on stones and had to stay behind, and the

shipments of supplies from the US also provided transportation back to the nearest cities for the injured and sick, so no one was ever left in the desert to die.

[21]And the army kept growing.

3

[1]Josue didn't know the images of the group were on the news in the United States every night in the month before their arrival. [2]While "migrant caravan" managed to be the most journalistic and most flattering description of the group, the blogosphere and even op-eds in respectable newspapers railed about the "invading hoard" and the "wave of illegals." [3]One writer indulged himself by calling them: "the disease-riddled mass of criminals, gang-bangers, rapist, murders, drug dealers, and thugs storming The Wall to collect welfare, take American jobs, and refuse to learn English." [4]This was incorrect, redundant, offensive, and ignorant, but none of those qualities would have prevented the description from achieving popularity in the United States. It was too long for Twitter, though, so it didn't catch on.

[5]When they arrived at The Wall, the gates were shut. [6]None of the usual traffic of 18 wheelers carrying autoparts and minivans carrying vacationing families could pass, so many of the commuters and truckers on the Mexican side of the border stepped out of their vehicles and joined with the caravan in a spontaneous

protest of the closure. [7]Josue had led the group to a spot where The Wall was a three story concrete barrier and not the steel slat/chainlink/razor wire fence that ran through much of the desert and along the shores of the Rio Grande. There, the crowd could have cut their way through or climbed over. [8]But here, outside Juarez, the Americans had decided to save money for one of their new detention centers by building only three sides and joining it directly to the fourth that was The Wall. [9]On the other side of all that concrete, children, some as young as infants, cared for one another by huddling in heaps of bodies under thin mylar blankets while border patrol agents shouted at them to stop crying. [10]Up on top of The Wall, some of these agents were joined by active duty soldiers of the army, violating the *pax comitate* by mere feet as they aimed their rifles down at the unarmed crowd below.

[11]A hush spread through the crowd as Josue walked toward The Wall. [12]A voice on a bullhorn shouted a warning in heavily accented Gringo Spanish telling the migrants to disperse, and that attempts to climb The Wall would result in arrest. [13]As a last warning, the soldiers turned on laser sights which lit up Josue with dozens of dancing, demonic fireflies flitting all over his body, trying to find his center as he walked.

[14]Josue did not hesitate, but he didn't hurry, either. [15]He'd mastered one pace across the desert, and he maintained it as he stepped up to the windowless slab of concrete

that climbed to the soldiers above him. [16]Gently, he placed his palm against The Wall, pressed, felt its solidity and his own arrival. [17]Then he turned and walked back twenty meters into the crowd and, in the same quiet voice always used, he delivered the orders of the angel of the Lord.

[18]The first pass was hard for the guards atop the prison wall to even see. [19]At different speeds, the people of the migrant caravan started walking to the west, but because they lacked any quick system of communication, there was a lot of confusion as word spread through the massive group. The guards thought maybe the whole army had given up and was headed off to some other point of entry. [20]But Josue led them only some three hundred meters away, down to where the concrete wall was only two stories because it didn't double as the fourth side of a detention center. [21]Then he stopped, gave the crowd a bit of time to catch up, and started walking back to the east. [22]A clamor of thousands of hushed voices percolated up from the crowd as the confused people heard the orders they'd missed, but soon everyone had been informed, and now the crowd marched silently, at every step closer together and closer to The Wall, but still heading east along its face. [23]Then, some six hundred meters away on the east side, Josue stopped, turned, and began walking back.

[24]The whole migrant caravan followed suit, and the guards watched in utter incomprehension as ten

thousand people marched back and forth on the other side of The Wall, behind the detention center, six times. [25]On the seventh, the guards could feel the change in the crowd. Far more eyes were turned up at them, and though the crowd was still mostly silent, many were tapping one another on the shoulder and gesturing excitedly. [26]More than one guard put his finger into the trigger guard of his rifle and aimed the laser scope into the crowd when he spotted some of the men pulling long, cylindrical tubes out of bags, but these were bumpy and transparent and unlike any weapons they'd ever seen, so they hesitated.

[27]Josue stopped right in the middle of the rear wall of the detention center and raised his arm. Some of the migrants followed suit, though the guards could tell they were unsure; this part of the ceremony hadn't been made clear to them, either. [28]Then Josue lowered his arm in a quick motion, like he was starting a drag race, even bending at the knees a bit to accentuate the arc of his arm. The others holding up their arms did the same. [29]Now the men holding the cylindrical tubes they'd cut and melted out of the donated plastic water bottles pressed their lips to the mouths of their homemade instruments and blew into them, trumpet-style, with all their might. [30]The sound of each instrument was something like a vuvuzela mixed with a didgeridoo, but it was more like a loud, low fart. Even multiplied by a thousand, this comparison was inescapable. [31]Nothing is more universally comic than the sound of a fart. It

transcends language and culture. [32]Any human with an orifice which can make that sound, either accidentally or on purpose, can bring a smile to the face of any other human. [33]The guards atop The Wall, hearing this massive flatulent noise, rediscovered a bit of the humanity they shed when scowling at frightened children, and they laughed.

[34]They would have been wiser to refrain.

[35]For just as nothing is more universally comic than the sound of a fart, nothing sparks anger like the sound of grown men with weapons standing in high places laughing at the bedraggled people they oppress. [36]When Josue raised his arm again, the watching trumpeters fell immediately silent, but the guards did not, and now the sounds of their laughter echoed over the heads of the migrants. [37]Laughter is contagious, but only to a point. The stifled giggles of some guards and soldiers had spread through the ranks atop The Wall, and now they could hardly help themselves. [38]Some were using the laughter as a weapon against their own discomfort. Others wanted to let their comrades know they were all on the same side against the evil hoard below. And others wanted to combat the very real fear they felt in that moment by attacking the migrants with their derision. [39]This was a mistake. [40]For the bullied do not laugh with the bullies. [41]The contagion of laughter is not that strong. [42]So while Josue held up his hand that second time, 20,000 eyes watched him in silence, listening to the sound of that

laughter, and burning.

[43]Then Josue brought down his arm again. [44]Without the guard's laughter, perhaps the migrants would have hesitated. [45]Someone would have shouted, and others would have followed, and the migrants would have looked to one another for permission to follow the order the little Guatelmalteco said came from the angel of the Lord. [46]But after listening to that laughter, they were primed, so when Josue dropped his arm, 10,000 people aimed all their rage at The Wall and shouted as loudly as they could. [47]The shouts were a wordless wave of fury. [48]Some of the migrants covered their ears as they screamed, but others, out of spite or curiosity or fellow-feeling, choose to hear the sound. [49]Eardrums ruptured and blood ran down the sides of their heads. [50]Children went from shouting to wailing at the pain in their ears. [51]Some people were deafened forever. [52]The works of the Lord are terrible to behold.

[53]When the sound hit The Wall, the cinderblock structure rumbled briefly and then collapsed before the guards standing on top had a chance to move. [54]A three story fall into rubble killed most of them, and even the survivors weren't laughing anymore. [55]When that section of The Wall came down, it twisted the rebar inside enough to create another wave, this one moving east and west. [56]It was a wave of incompetence and greed; the contractors who built The Wall had done so in the style they'd been taught by the President. [57]Shoddy supplies, poor

workmanship, and the right campaign contributions make for much higher profits than building to last, so it was hardly miraculous that the entire wall fell at once. [58]Metal slats snapped and knocked into one another like dominoes, their rusted bases groaning and cracking as they went. [59]Chain link rippled as it chose a side of the border upon which to lay down and die. [60]Cheap concrete pulverized to sand. [61]From San Diego, California, to the Las Palomas Wildlife Management Area in the Texan portion of the Gulf of Mexico, the fences and barriers and divides of all kinds that made up The Wall quickly, loudly, and dramatically transformed into 1,945 miles of futility and garbage.

[62]The far more miraculous effect of the event CNN dubbed "The Shout" (and twitter and Instagram labeled "#shout") was witnessed in far flung regions of the US. [63]Starting in Texas and spreading in a semi-circular arc across the whole nation, the walls of all the other concentration camps set up for housing those accused of violating immigration laws also fell. [64]Razorwire snapped and coiled in on itself like an invitation to pass. [65]Windows cracked and crumbled without exploding onto the prisoners. [66]Many of the guards were injured and no small number were killed as their prisons collapsed around them, but none of the captured migrants suffered a scratch.

[67]After The Shout, all across the country at these sites, a deep silence reigned. [68]Veronica, godmother to Josue's

daughter Cecilia, touched her son Little Emilio on the shoulder, pushing him towards Josue. [69]Despite his name, Little Emilio was taller than his own father and towered above Josue, though his lanky frame and shuffling gait now projected his uncertainty. [70]"Now what, Josue?" he asked. "Where did the angel of the Lord say we were to go next?"

[71]Josue had to reach up above his own shoulder to rest a gentle hand on the young man's. [72]"Anywhere we want," he said.

[73]And then Josue started the 2003 mile journey back to Maria and his daughters.

[74]He walked alone. [75]The members of the caravan had intended to go into *El Norte*, and they did so. [76]The people flowing out of the concentration camps went east and west and north and south. [77]It didn't much matter to them. [78]They weren't escaping into the promised land. [79]For that was a secret the angel of the Lord had spoken to Josue which he did not share with the people, but which he confided to Maria and his daughters months later. [80]The United States was not a holy land, the angel told him. [81]It was a country like any other, and not God's favorite. [82]And when a country steals childhood from children, even when God sets them free, the land cannot be forgiven for the theft. [83]God's forgiveness is not that strong.

Thirteen Ways of Looking at a Black Bird

by Lydia K. Valentine

(after Wallace Stevens)

I

Among a crowd of jeering vultures,
the only still thing
was the grace of the Black bird.

II

I was of three minds,
like a tree where
three broken Black birds swing.

III

The Black bird whirls in the blast's wind.
It is a main part of the national pantomime.

IV

A Sister and a Brother
are one.
A Sister and a Brother and a Black bird
are one.

V

I do not know which to prefer,
the beauty of our shade
or the beauty of our subtlety,
the Black bird brewing tea
or just sipping?

VI

History fills the long window
with glass privilege.
The shadow of the Black bird
passes it, back and forth.
Denial etches
into the Shadow
a hidden rage.

VII

O haughty vessels of Babel,
why do you cling to lacquered binaries?
Do you not see how the Black birds
fly above you, reflecting every
hued letter of the rainbow?

VIII
I know towering ivory dialect
and corset-tight diction;
but I know, too,
that Black bird vernacular
is at the heart of all I know.

IX
After the Black bird fell,
chalk marked the edges
of one more outline.

X
At the sight of Black birds
kneeling in flashing lights,
even the mothers of strangers
should cry out sharply.

XI
He walked from 7-11
in a herald's cowl.
Bullets, not fear, pierced him
when another mistook
the purpose of *his* equipage:
slaying Black birds.

XII
The river is moving.
A Black bird must be dying.

XIII
It was sundown all morning.
It was raining,
and it was going to rain.
The Black bird nested
in the cedar box.

The Tides of Macon

by Zack Dye

The strings that outlined the former body peeked above a few inches of water on the side street. A woman peered from behind the crack of her doorway there on the bottom floor of an apartment entryway. The police detectives started using string to mark the location of any homicide victims because the rain and tides would quickly wash away any chalk they used to use to draw on the ground. Too often the beaches there in Macon, Georgia would give way to large tides that would flood the streets of the Southern town for several hours every day. There was no way chalk would keep.

Momma continued to stare through the door onto the dark flooded Macon street. She could see her son's outline there in the street, the little sticks and string popping up from the water below. She saw the policemen coming up the street, so she kept the door open, waiting for them to arrive.

"Eve Mann? That is you, correct?"

"Evelyn, Sir, but please, just Momma. Everyone just calls me Momma." She looked briefly at the men's badges. Water dripped from the men's sleeves and onto their outstretched badges. Momma just motioned for them to come in. She parted the door and led the large men inside. Once their coats were hung behind the door and the water stamped off their rain boots they sat down.

"You called the station, Ma'am? We were doing more investigation on the death. Apologies. But they told us you wanted to give us some new information?" The detectives looked around the house. A cracked viewer screen sat in the corner. An empty cabinet behind the slightly ajar cabinet door was visible in the kitchen. Water stains notched the lower part of the walls where an occasional flood crept in.

"Just before Michael was found out...side." Momma choked very briefly, revisiting the pain. She apologized, then continued, "There were several guys out there. They were wearing all their gear, and the water was high. They were out in the middle of the street, so you can check all the surveillance video. But people were wading everywhere and a couple flatbottoms passed in the street. I know they all had their Pulsators with them. So, who knows what may have exactly happened, but no doubt one thing led to another and then someone *had to use their damn Pulsator*. They *always* do."

Her voice was steady but the tone shrill in its anger.

"But afterwards I saw someone come back to the area, as if they were going back to the body. Some kid was walking up and down and across the street just looking at me when I was standing outside with Mike dead there."

"A kid, Ma'am?" The shorter, older detective was doing all the questioning.

"Yeah, he was creeping around and just looking at me weird. I'm sure you'll see it in the surveillance vids."

"We're looking now - there's a lot of footage. Also, there were quite a few strikes that night. I'm sure you noticed the power cutting out a few times... But, Momma," he put his hand on her shoulder, same height as his trying to reassure her, "we're going through all the other points. We have everyone's geo-coordinates, we know who was there, we think. We have the video. But since each Pulsator has a unique code for activation and also has a required geo-coordinate tracker, we feel we just need to find the device that did this."

"All those boys, they were just out front. But it was like this kid was coming back for something. I couldn't get a look at him because he was in waders with his synthhoodie all the way over his head."

"Mrs. Mann, that's not a terrific description but trust me, we'll be getting to the video surveillance very shortly to see whatever we might also have there. We're trying to check all geo-coordinated activity in the area first - phones, Pulsators, biotrackers, whatever they might have had amongst their devices. We hope from there the video can confirm other data points."

"Well, I hope so, too. I hope so, too."

"Thank you for calling us back. We're going to continue to surveil the area for any other clues now that we have more daylight. But we'll connect with you as we have anything further."

A tear came to Mrs. Mann's eye as she reopened the door for them. She closed the door before checking the shelf by the door. The drawer was closed. The keys were in order. Michael had an extra pack of synthetic tobacco he liked to smoke there on the table. She wondered if they had noticed it. But she took it and put it neatly in the drawer there. Beneath the table, his indoor slippers were paired together with all the other dry-climate/indoor footwear.

The downtown area was like any former tourist town. Back when the oceans had finally claimed Florida, Southern Georgia filled as the water crept inland over the peninsula and panhandle. This was many years ago, almost a century at this point, in fact. Now the town succumbed to the ills of many other once "boom" towns. Miami, the original tourist haven of the American Carribean, was evacuated these days - the buildings now buried by melted polar ice. The panhandle quickly disappeared as the oceans crept into Alabama and on towards the foothills of the Adirondacks. Birmingham was now one of the busiest cities in the world. The former industrial town was now a tourist paradise with newly tropical golf courses and ocean towns as near as Tuscaloosa. The airport hummed with people coming for vacation... to "fun in the sun." Communities were changed dramatically by these quickly shifting demands.

The tides had crept in on Macon as they had many other towns caught literally in the rising tide of the world's oceans. As the tides rose and the climate zones changed, the world's supply chains were also quickly reconstituted. The largest effect of these changes was food supply. As the Sahara humidified, it nevertheless proved unable to support agriculture. South American jungles had long since been burned to the ground, first for agriculture, then for cities. The American plains would now flood regularly making crop planning and harvesting an absolutely unpredictable nightmare for the farmers in that region.

The Pacific Northwest had managed quite well, its rich soil reacted well to more humid and warm conditions. The tundra of Russia also yielded many staples given its vast expanse and previously untilled ground. But these were exceptions amidst the catastrophes of late 21st century climate change. As the planet population increased, food shortage was vastly more widespread. Inflation skyrocketed as land values diminished heavily in rural areas: uninhabitable and unworkable. In the Southern United States, the best industry became tourism. This was the way out. Inflate any and all prices and local taxes as tourists came to vacation. Everybody likes a day at the beach, everybody - inelastic demand as economists might say. Everyone got everything they could-before the rising tides swallowed new little cities whole. Eventually torrents of hurricanes would surge during a season, some season, and then the water would not recede. The town would remain barely inhabitable, but the tourism would quickly die after those floods would not recede. The captains of hospitality would take the money from their hotels or casinos and head higher up shore, literally "to dry land."

Whenever this would happen, those without means to move would get stuck, a generation or two of families built on the town's fleeting commercial success. As the money and jobs left town, cities would be left with the expected issues: underfunded schools, underfunded infrastructure maintenance, underfunded health care. Consequently, people wouldn't finish school, as if there were jobs anyway after the tides refused to ebb, and naturally any black market medicines would do. As with all back markets, particularly for meds and pills (anything that could bring cheap relief), crime and poverty would seize these communities. And in towns like this, towns like Macon, Georgia in the late 2200s, murder would be rampant, and the victims would almost appreciate the ensuing relief of death.

The deaths accelerated as the money left. The rampant drug use in the destitute town left the vulnerable more vulnerable. The problem wasn't so much enforcement of illicit drug use. Rehabilitation programs were prevalent. If anyone was caught with anything illegal, they were likely just sent to rehabilitation centers closer to Atlanta. But often the damage was done well before then. Zombied junkies could do far more damage among themselves than the police could. And so the deaths and murders escalated rapidly among drug users looking for a way out of the poor and depressing circumstances, just looking for the next "score," the tiniest moments of relief.

Originally, the Macon police response was draconian, like the efforts from the 21st century. In the south those had persisted well into next century. Private prisons made sure Macon's police force dragged in as many suspects as possible. Local district attorneys would prosecute to the full extent they could. Judges would throw the book as far as they could at any suspects. But with the epidemic increasing, the chalk outlines were almost literally everywhere. They would rest in doorsteps or on street meridians. They were found on sidewalks but also elevators - where drug dealing and drug use was easily more covert. Between these outlines strewn about the city's passageways amidst the increasing tidewaters, police were forced to stop using chalk. The water would just wash away evidence of the precise location of a person's death. Now they used the string outlines which sat above the tides. And they could be seen throughout Macon, like little tombstones where ever you might look, even staircases, parking lots, parks, front lawns, rooftops, and in this case, the middle of the street. Macon's citizenry had certainly become desensitized to the death that was washing in with the tides.

Saturdays were very busy out on the streets where Momma lived. She watched the kids come and go through the late afternoon and through the big storm that washed through that evening. There was a thunderstorm and brief blackouts for a couple minutes here and there, no more than 3 or 4 though. The local electric company had been struggling to keep up infrastructure, and so little hits of lightning could put down the electricity for a couple minutes while the central grid was reset to provide backup. When the power went out like that, the kids became unpredictable - sometimes they scattered, sometimes they didn't. They were the same junkies that she saw all the time and you never quite knew what they'd do. They were all friends of Mike's though. She had seen their faces up close and aplenty. They had names that would wash over her when Mike would tell her about them. Mike and those kids were in it together. The whole neighborhood suffered from the same epidemic, and the ones who survived couldn't help but know each other somehow. She was deep in reflection, thinking about *all* of their time aboard this sinking ship of a city.

"I don't know, Momma, they just do it," Michael said to his mother trying to explain why he needed the money. "They fix the Pulsator so that it don't track, it don't register. Ma, this is the only way I'm gonna be able to protect myself and keep myself safe... Look at this way:

They literally won't even know it's here."

"It's a lot of money. You been taking a lot these days. I've got my own meds I gotta keep around. I hardly eat cuz you been taking everything to get fixes and..."

"I know, I been a real pain in the ass." His hands twitched as he talked. Momma could see he hadn't had a fix in a while. She felt for him. She really did. "But Ma, you gotta understand that this is really a special situation. This keeps us both safe."

She went for her money box she kept hidden. It had the cash in it for things that cards wouldn't purchase, like a modified Pulsator that wouldn't track or register - just kill. She came back out and pulled out the money and handed it to Mike. That was much earlier in the day; he had left much earlier on the day he'd died. Sometime in the misty morning light, he had taken that cash out to one of those same tweakers out in the street. She watched Mike hand over the cash *and* his Pulsator ("The only real protection you can have," the kids would say). After that exchange, everyone dispersed in their own directions. She watched Mike head over to a market to get a new pack of synthetic tobacco that he was always smoking. That was probably better. It seemed to calm his nerves even for just short periods of time. She turned back into the house to listen to some music while she made some toast. She was eating a lot of toast and oatmeal these days. No butter or brown sugar, just toast and oatmeal most days.

The problem was that Michael could not break his cycle. He was always clever enough to not get arrested.

He was somehow at the wrong place at the right time so that nothing ever stuck to him. Ultimately though, there was never enough to satisfy him. This was, of course, the disease of addiction and poverty. His belly was empty and his nerves were always wracked. The only surprise was how everything could just disappear. Meds, food... and oh, the money.

The money was never safe. That box she kept, she knew Michael knew about it. He tried desperately not to touch it, and that was their strange bargain. He could take from the house: food, stronger pain relief medications that were prescribed to his mother, the room he lived in for free. And he would ask for money as well. If she could, Momma would give him some on occasion.

After looking at the window, watching Michael hand over that money, she started to think about the box. In closing the box, she felt that the box was very light. That Michael, maybe even unknowingly, had taken money from the cash box in one of his stupors when Momma was gone. She knew this was not her child that would do this. This was a fiend that needed more and more. Of course, she had supposed this time would come. She had prayed that it would not. But suddenly, shortly after she sent him off to modify the Pulsator, she came more clearly to the realization that his body was fully infected.

Maybe earlier, a few years ago, a few months ago, Michael would been aware enough have said something about at least taking the money. But in a mostly dilapidated house with only bread and oats because of all

Michael's thieving from his own mother, this was taking the last she had. When she checked the box to find that he had taken a noticeable amount of money earlier, she felt more violated than she ever had - even in this neighborhood, town and catastrophe that had claimed her and her son's lives, she had reached a breaking point.

Momma frequently reminisced on the younger days. They both worked. Michael was vibrant and joyous. He was her baby. Even as the waters began rising and the businesses were starting to notice the inevitable, Michael and his momma had managed fine. "You going to make it to school this afternoon?" she asked him one afternoon.

"I hope so. After I let you off, I have to run an errand or two and then head off to school. But yes, I'll make it in time." He smiled at her. His long face squirmed with a happy delight. He had always been a fidgety child. Even at school, where he was receiving special help, his teachers said it was hard to keep him focused. But Momma did everything she could to get him through. And after high school, one of the technical schools had him on a training program to be a Casino Tech. He would be able to help manage the gambling machines, their algorithms, and any other issues with which the casinos might need help.

She saddened when she remembered how happy he seemed then. She didn't realize that it was in those days that his early use had begun. Before class he would sneak a few drinks with friends. He was hooked on smoking Finka, a strange combination of pleasure drug and pain killer. This was only the beginning. She would find small glass vials in the trash at home as he became less discreet. She knew what they were. She didn't know the kind of drug, but she knew it was drugs. He moved from there to synthetic morphine.

The opioid epidemic from the early 21st century had become something different, but the need for painkillers was omnipresent. Humans throughout history have lusted for anything to kill the pain. As the tidal patterns changed and the world devolved into a hungrier place with fewer farms and crops, poppies and opioid production also suffered. If one couldn't literally eat a crop, the crop often ceased to exist. In this vein, synthetic opioids, especially morphine, became quite fashionable - because it was also considered eco-friendly. In fact, synthetic morphine seemed harmless enough in the early days that doctors were paid handsomely by the rich to administer the drug. The reason it seemed so harmless was, under doctor supervision, abuse was somehow curtailed. The price was also prohibitive because of the requirement to employ a doctor.

Unfortunately, this made a town like Macon especially susceptible to an overflow of a drug like this.

Rich people flew in from all over to employ casino doctors, doctors required to be licensed and approved. These wealthy tourists wanted to spend synthetic vacations in the sun, near the water. Virtual reality and sensory deprivation tanks allowed people a fully falsified reality in the safety of their hotel rooms and in the presence of a doctor. When the medical and virtual experience was over, guests would go to the pool or to the nearby shores and casually rest in the sun. The alternating sensory realities became very popular. When Macon was at its tourist peak, one of its main attractions was travel packages for these intermingled: "Morphine/Virtual Realities." Inevitably, these drugs leaked into the general population. A popular drug is never something that can be extinguished. Even after several centuries, types of alcohol and tobacco were both still widely in circulation. Despite their ill effects, people loved the experience of drinking and smoking. So the governments had little choice but to regulate this new addition and hope to manage public health in the face of any dangers to those taking it.

As the tides became a greater and greater threat to Macon and its tourism industry, the casinos did leave. Cash and jobs became scarce. These were certainly contributing factors to Michael's fall. As he initially experimented with drugs and alcohol, the education he was receiving became less valuable. He graduated and hoped to work quietly with the casinos as a Tech and start a nice life, but the casino jobs vanished. Rather than any routine or success with work he might've had, Michael was forced, like many his age, to literally do nothing. He could go around town looking for work, but the technical degrees that he and other kids like him had worked for were gone. And there he was, broke, hungry, at home with his mother - both of them looking for opportunity.

Things only got worse. One night Momma came home and found Michael on the floor. He was seizing on the ground and had vomited in his mouth. He was face up and choking on his own vomit. She quickly cleared his mouth and grabbed the home respirator that was with the other basic first aid equipment. She'd previously worked as a pediatric nurse, so she knew the value in having one of these. She had seen many parents come in to the hospitals after drug use. These small portable devices could help people respirate in any form of consciousness. As Michael's drug use increased over time, she brought a cheap one home just in case - for just this occasion.

While having to do this broke her heart, the episode seemed to have *also* broken Michael's pride. He became more withdrawn and found more ways to numb his pain. Alcohol, synthetic morphine, synthetic tobacco, Finka, and on occasion he would take his mother's high-dose pain killers that she had been prescribed for her back - chronic pain that she'd started getting after Michael was born but which stayed with her after that. The long nights and long shifts over the years continued to aggravate her back. She took the medicine as prescribed and as needed. As Michael's drug addiction continued, when she wasn't looking, Michael would sneak in for a fix and take whatever he needed in that moment. It all became a disaster. The jobs were gone. The streets were flooded. The city was crumbling. And the kids were all addicted to drugs.

When her doctor laid her off about a year before, she wasn't sure how she was going to go forward. Even with the meager US Basic Income she was receiving, it was a far cry from her salary at the pediatrician's office. But as the wealthy families and their children fled, there was nothing to be done, no amount of supply will satisfy a total lack of demand. After that, there was nothing extra in the house, of anything, no luxury - not for Michael and not for Momma. Just quiet days passing time, trying to do with less and less.

"Momma, he just had to remove the base plate here. Then the tracker chip is here. The DNA coder imprint is on the other side." He turned over the Pulsator hastily. He was still breathing heavily with excitement. Remembering some of his own early tech training days on standard government regulation licenses implanted into the software. "The DNA coder imprint registers a pulse after the victim is hit. And that kicks to the local geo-coordinate register in the area. A server, a traffic light, a street light, somebody's wrist comm or even just their earpiece. That's why we have to have this stuff removed. But since the government software requires a back-end shut-off of the code, you have to go to the black market to find a coder who will shut that off. They did the same thing with the gaming machines for the casinos we used to learn about."

"I don't care. You need help, Son. I just want you alive. But I don't think anything will help ... you took money from the cash box, dammit. I told you never to take money from the cash box." She had been waiting for him to come back, in hopes he might confess to taking all the money she found missing just a few hours ago. She needed him to admit to anything.

As Michael continued, Momma looked around. First the cabinets caught her eye. A couple across the faded kitchen island. She knew there was nothing inside them. The rusted 3D food printer they used for quite a few years just stood there - meaningless as an empty promise. She couldn't afford to buy the more quality ingredients needed to run the food printer. She felt the hunger in her belly, the pain of the times she wouldn't eat as she left Michael a few bucks for his own needs.

Then a glance over to the entertainment screen. They were so excited when she brought it home. A Christmas gift from her boss. That was only a couple Christmases ago when times were still good. Even though things were already in pretty serious decline and the waters had risen and tourists were harder to find, things were still manageable with Momma working at the doctor's office. In the worsening Macon condition, that screen kept them both entertained on many nights through their troubles. Then, one night, Michael came home, stumbling from alcohol and Finka, and he knocked the screen to the floor as he fell on his face. The screen cracked but still worked. Now, though, every time she saw the crack, the frustration picked at her. Tonight, it enraged her. The empty, dingy moldy bottom floor of the apartment - she held so much contempt for it all.

"When some fool tries to move on me, I just take the Pulsator like this:..." Michael was still demonstrating the best way to use the weapon. She was exhausted by all of this. "Then you take it here between any point of contact with the skin and it immediately sends a fully charged pulse of nuclear electricity to the heart and the base of the brain, basically pulverizing both on impact. The charge connects through the spine which acts as a conduit and fries a guy. You just push that button right there when the safety is turned off like this." He pressed a red button. Then he turned the Pulsator back over and showed her the blue button on the palm side of the handle. He handed over the weapon to his mother so she could look at it as if she were his partner in crime.

She looked back at him, his desperate skinny eyes looking back at her from dull apartment colors in the background. His hollowed face on top of his sinewy neck shaking like a broken jack in the box. At that moment the apartment went dark. The lightning darkened the neighborhood, and she felt the Pulsator in her hand. The emptiness of everything, from the apartment to her stomach to the burned-out lights of her son's addicted soul - the void of everything seized on her, and she pushed the weapon into Michael's neck and put pressure on the blue button in her palm. He collapsed to the ground just as he said a victim would - internal nuclear combustion of the heart and base of the brain. Her anger overwhelmed all her maternal instincts. She grabbed the body in the darkness, still warm and limp before the rigor. Opening the door, she dragged his body quickly across the sidewalk and into the middle of the damp street. She left him there and slipped back into her house in the darkness, putting the Pulsator in the drawer of the table by the door. Just as she closed the drawer and locked the door, the lights came back on. The frantic episode had taken just a couple minutes. She had barely realized she'd done any of it.

She collapsed on the couch, mechanically turned on the cracked screen, and stared at the broken vision in front of her. She looked out the window, and a group of boys had gathered around the body. She saw one talking into his wrist comm. They all looked furtively around the neighborhood, scanning for anybody who might have just left a body in the middle of the dark. Momma let the slightly open curtain swing back across the window, falling between her face and the glass. Turning back to the flickering, cracked screen, she closed her eyes. She knew where she was. She didn't know what she'd done. She could only sleep.

The police came back two days later and knocked on

Momma's door again. She cracked the door but did not let them in this time. "We just wanted to reconnect Mrs. Mann," the shorter, older officer began. "We looked at all the tape in the area and we didn't see anyone lurking around the neighborhood."

"My eyes can be a little tricky sometimes," she said back solemnly. "I don't know. I guess that's why I wanted the video checked."

"Mrs. Mann, honestly, we have a lot of homicides in Macon. And we don't often find too many of the killers. The Pulsators, we're sure that's what killed your son, a lot of them have been modified. So it's a weapon our junkies like to use, and nowadays they can be fixed so they are untrackable."

"Junkies." The word settled on her inflamed heart. The nothingness in the officers voice, just like the moment she had actually killed her son.

"If one of them has modified one of the Pulsators, they are hard to find. Not to mention the power was off for several minutes before your son just appeared in the street. This happens frequently. Murders happen and then people put the body in a truck waiting for the electricity to go off. Then they dump the body when they know there is no surveillance. We're tracking the automobiles that were in the area around the time the electricity went off." A tear streamed down her cheek. "I'm sorry, Mrs. Mann. If we can get a track on the weapon, we can find the killer. That could be tough, though. We're going to check the neighborhood one more time for our report. We're very sorry. We're very,

very sorry for your loss."

The officer seemed sincere as he apologized. She shed another tear and motioned politely for them to leave. She could see that, for the time being, the street was dry. The police left the doorway. Momma looked at the table next to the door. Then she looked at the string outline out in the street. Finally, she closed the door after the officers had left. She opened the drawer in the table. Inside lay a pack of Michael's synthetic tobacco and his modified Pulsator, the one she had used to kill her son. A hunger pulled at her belly. She closed the drawer, felt an awkward smile ease across the bottom of her face, and went to eat a piece of dry toast.

comparatives

by Rebecca Smolen

we watch the whales die
in large numbers, with sudden force
that the other ocean animals do not have
time to eat what remains, to destroy
evidence that humans will continue
to murder. even seagulls don't want
more than a nibble.

at such a speed women become
a closer parallel with incubator
made of comparable parts and gears and
correct atmosphere to grow more humans,
more hunters, predators, parasites

we watch the whales die.
they wash ashore muscle-wasted,
sunken eyes clenched, lids puckered with
permanent furrow from a world searched
found barren of fulfillment.

women held guilty when
pregnancy is unwanted or unviable.
rulings as dagger hover right above
her fault, ready to plunge. to prevent
those indictments a man-made law will
remove choice, remove rational thought
remove emotion as if we are not mammals too.

the whales die
in a state of panic with
no energy to panic. shriveled
to bones under starved skin atop
carcass bloated only with *our* guilt
others don't want to feed on.
no blubber unused to flense
for leather, candles or lipstick.

women best as host, a husk when
aged, dried out, no longer useful, wrung
and twisted around themselves for every
energy they could provide. then
tossed like compost with other
broken bits, rejected, to be forgotten.

we watch the whales die.
death warmed by blood that dribbles over
features that make them mammals like us, when
a newborn calf dies a mother whale carries her body

at the surface of the water for 17 days as if the air might
reach her lungs, to mourn, unlike us, unknowing
as far as we know, of what *we* do to them
or would there be distinction
if they were aware?

Hope for a Green Hero

by Eric Witchey

Dieter froze at the cabin door, his knuckles turning white on the cedar latch. Instinctual certainty told him his grandfather lurked behind him in a shadowy corner. The glowmold lantern in Dieter's other hand swung forward then back, clinking softly.

"One." Grandpa Franz's sanding block voice scraped at Dieter's spine. "Just one day in Oregon." The short hairs on Dieter's neck stood to attention. "Now, you figure you can poach alone?"

Dieter sucked in a reeking breath of stale old man and illegal wood smoke. Hand still on the latch, he spoke to the door. "One day watching your pathetic scrounging is enough. You can't teach me anything."

"Poaching ain't easy on a veteran's reservation."

Dieter turned and peered into the darkness. The hiss of labored breathing and the dry creak of Grandpa Franz's willow rocker marked the shadowy corner where the old man had lain in ambush. Dieter hung his lantern from a hook on an overhead beam. The dancing pale green light still didn't reveal Grandpa Franz, but the swinging circle of light did reveal the archaic double-bladed axe Franz used as a cane. The old blade was against rough-hewn floorboards it had probably been used to cut. The long, slightly curved handle leaned against the log wall.

"You offering help?" Dieter asked.

The old man's hacking cough sounded like the death rattle of a pre-war logging truck. "Your Pa teach you to steal?"

"And took nothing of yours."

"You're wearing my sawyer's uniform."

Dieter pulled up the hood of the war surplus, Lumberman issue protective coverall and squared off against the shadows. "You ain't usin' it."

"Guess I ain't."

"You ain't brung nothing down in years."

"Don't take what I don't need."

Dieter squinted, trying to see the old man's twisted face in the shadows. "Everything you got come off the forest floor," Dieter said. "War hero or not, Pa was twice the poacher you ever was."

"Dead twice as good as alive?" The chair creaked. Franz's face appeared, a sickly gray-green shade in the swaying lamplight. Dark scars made his skin look like mangled Doug Fir bark. Faded eyes the color of greenish-white smoke held Dieter's heart still for a beat.

Franz reached for the axe. That mangled hand was a legend in the family. Dieter's belly tightened. The twisted thumb, two nubbin stumps, and his two smallest fingers reached out and gripped the handle.

"They caught Pa by accident," Dieter said.

Franz used the axe to help him stand. "He set no perimeter alarms. That ain't an accident. That's fatal stupid."

"He didn't waste away hiding in the dark."

"You got his blood in you, boy."

"And yours."

Franz ignored Dieter, and old-man shuffled across the dusty cabin floor until he was so close Dieter shied away from his liquor and dead meat breath. "Goin' out for meat or money, boy?"

Dieter closed his eyes against the foul breath and the insulting sound of the word "boy." When he opened them, he looked down on the frail, hunched figure his family worshipped as a hero. Thin strands of yellowed white hair stretched between brown spots on Franz's pate. The suspenders of his threadbare overalls were tied in knots at the shoulders, replacing buckles that wore out ages ago.

Dieter's fear of discovery by a family legend melted. Cold contempt flowed into the space where his fear had been. "Money. More money than you made in your whole life, old man."

"Pride and greed." Franz said.

"Ambition. Hope."

"Yup. Got your Pa killed. Same blood."

"You didn't help him, either."

The old man nodded. The green light shone on his pate. "You coulda' followed in his footsteps. Coulda' raised a family poaching on the tree farms in Georgia. Instead, you come to the reservation. Why? An' don't tell me that money and ambition shit. There's easier ways for both."

Dieter stared in silent anger. The one day that had passed since he arrived seemed like weeks. "You don't know nothin'. If you ever did, you forgot."

Franz rapped the head of his axe on the dusty floorboards. "I tell you why," Franz rasped. "You believed them tree-killin' stories they tell about me. You come here to learn to hunt trees that don't stand in rows waitin' for the harvesters."

The truth of Franz's words set a flame to Dieter's dry anger. "Bullshit!" Dieter snapped. "Them stories was lies. You never fought for human rights. You got all them scars in a car wreck or. . ." He trailed off. The old man's deep, sad eyes wouldn't let him believe his own words. The scars were too real, too deep.

"The trees ain't going nowhere, boy. Get the true lay of things before you--"

"I can get in deep before sunrise, drop a giant, mill it, and sell it before sunset."

"Only trees out there big enough to satisfy you are veterans. They'll be standing long after you and me are dust."

Dieter thought maybe the old man's eyes misted up like he cared about Dieter.

"Them trees was designed to guard the old growth, boy. You don't know what they can do to a man." Franz touched his good hand to his scarred cheek. "They got tricks you--"

"You're scared," It wasn't caring that misted the old

man's eyes. "You don't poach 'cause you're scared."

"I made my peace with them, boy. I'm an old vet just like them."

"Mama would cry," Dieter said. "I don't believe this. You talk like they was people instead of eco-designed things."

"Sometimes," the old man's voice cracked. "Sometimes, I think they got more sense than some people."

"Sun's up in half an hour," Dieter said. "I got no time for fairy tales." He turned away from his grandfather and ran a finger up the seam of the uniform to seal it. "I gotta' go, Grampa."

"Course ya do," Franz rasped. "Just like your Pa. Can't take the time to save your own life."

Dieter ignored him. He wouldn't be baited by an old man. From a hook by the door, he grabbed the shoulder strap of the assault sawmill he inherited from his father.

Dieter slung the strap over his head. He settled the mill so the emitter muzzle pointed downward and the rifle stock and trigger guard rode against his hip. He laid his hand on the worn curve of the stock and let his trigger finger lay over the guard. His middle finger tapped reflexively at the safety.

"Join your Pa, then," Franz said. "You got the wantin' so bad you can't hear."

Dieter wondered what the sawmill would do to a man. Would it compute optimum usage and slice out planks and beams made of flesh and bone, or would the result be more like the pulpy mess the tree farm manager's boring tool had made of his father? He opened the cabin door.

"Keep the uniform," Franz said. "Saved my life more'n once. Maybe it'll keep you alive long enough to learn some sense."

Facing the predawn darkness, Dieter said, "Momma thinks you're some kind of old hero still out here fightin' the Green War."

"Your momma's wishin' for times that's gone. War's over for thirty years, boy. I'm a vet. I live on the res cause it's home. There's no place in the world for the likes of me."

"Gone because no one has the spine to fight." A cold, pine-scented coastal wind whipped in, slapped his face, and brought tears to his eyes.

Franz shuffled up behind him. A strong, two-fingered hand grasped his shoulder. "You're all full of juice-- hungry with pride and dreams." The smell of dead meat, tobacco, and scotch mingled with the pine wind. "You think there's glory in bringing down a big ol' war tree."

Dieter shrugged off the hand. "You gone soft, but Pa taught me right and proud."

"Dieter." Franz's voice was soft and low. The old man pulled on his shoulder until he turned and looked into his grandfather's pale eyes and tortured face. "If you gotta' go, take my axe. That mill your pa left you is fine for farm trees, but it'll just piss off the vets."

Dieter looked at the ancient blade and wooden handle. He pitied his grandfather. No one in their right mind would get close enough to a war tree to use an axe.

He shouldered his sawmill, crossed the threshold into the cold night, and closed the door on his grandfather. He touched the control at his collar to set his suit temperature and camouflage his heat signature. Then, he headed into the dense forest of the West Coast Veteran's Reservation.

Sunrise found Dieter pressing his eye to the cold eyepiece of his sights. The cross hairs automatically adjusted for distance, focusing just above the base of the biggest Sitka Spruce he'd ever seen. Hidden by his suit and still a safe two hundred meters from the tree, Dieter watched a shiny, black carpenter ant picking its way along vertical canyons of black and rust bark then across the circular, tarred scab of a pruned limb. Including the long, searching feelers and the massive mandibles, the ant was at least 20 millimeters long. Probably another nasty ecotech mutation.

Neither the ant, nor the fact that some tree-hugger had managed to prune and patch a war tree, mattered. He smiled. To the tree in his sights, he whispered his father's poaching mantra. "A logger's pride is skill and will."

The old coward had been right about one thing. Pa forgot his alarms. The farm manager stumbled on him milling out a kill. The green-brained SOB pulped pa with a forester's core bore. It was a humiliating thing to die at the wrong end of a tool made for sampling tree sap and cells.

Dieter was smarter. He wasn't taking chances—especially not on the veteran's reservation. His alarms were set. Anything taller than a cougar kitten moved on the ground inside a four-kilometer grid and a chime would sound in his ear.

Today, it would be just him and the tree. No interruptions. No surprises.

The sun warmed the forest fast. Steam rose in smoke-like tendrils through slanted god rays of sunlight. Settled in among benign sword ferns and dense clumps of rhododendron, he was alone with the Sitka.

The silver disk of a VA skybot whirred past above the forest canopy on a tireless patrol. Dieter automatically ducked for cover in spite of the uniform. He told himself that was fine. Who knew how well the old tech worked now, keeping veterans in the reservation and keeping people without permit transponders, people like Dieter, out?

Dieter pinched the temp adjustment on his collar. No way he'd let his external heat shift away from forest ambient more than a ten thousandth of a degree. No skybot was gonna' make and bake him.

Even grandpa Franz, that yellow-skinned, weak-willed, bark-faced old puke, would respect him when he brought down this grandmother Sitka.

Pa had warned him about hunting on the reservation, about war trees and their root attacks, about explosive chlorochem pinecones, fatal needles, and about pollen that could lacquer your lungs, choke you to death, and start breaking you down for fertilizer before you died. The Sitka was old and tall and she fit the description. She had put her roots down at the base of a black, south-facing basalt cliff that would both warm and protect her. Between her and Dieter, she commanded a clear half-circle of sloping meadow as wide as she was tall. Grass and flowers and sun surrounded her, and Dieter would have bet that nothing larger than a mouse lived inside that kill zone.

Even though he was still two hundred meters out and camouflaged, Dieter worked his way over to a ravine filled with mossy basalt boulders. The rocks offered more safety from root attack than open ground. The walls of the ravine protected his flanks, and one end of the ravine opened onto the clearing. From that opening, he'd have a clear, safe shot.

Dieter scanned the sky before he peeled back the index and middle fingers of his suit glove. He flipped off the sawmill's safety. Grandma Sitka's circumference at breast height was almost five meters. He did the CBH-to-board-meter conversion in his head. He sucked in a long breath. She'd bring twenty million. He'd flash that in front of the sorry old shit hiding in his smelly cabin.

He'd fell her on her right side where the ground was near enough level and clear of rocks that might lever her and damage the heartwood. If he milled her quick and camoed the lumber, he'd have a couple days to call in a fence and get her removed. It would take that long for the forest rangers to compare aerial photos and realize she was missing.

One knee on cold stone, he steadied the saw and let the computer register his cut plan. He slipped his finger off the guard and onto the trigger.

His sights filled with a white-pink blur.

Dieter pulled back from the sights.

He blinked and rubbed his eyes.

A woman stood at the base of his tree.

He set his eye back to the sights and refocused. She was his age. Her face was long and her eyes dark and sad. Her hair was free, long, dark, and billowing like Spanish moss in a breeze. It teased at breasts covered in a torn, red flannel shirt. He moved the cross hairs along the curve of her hips and down the straight edge of her khaki pants. New-grown roots covered her worn hiking boots. The tree had her.

The skybot had ignored her. She must be a hiker. Must have a permit transponder.

Served her right for wandering off the trails.

He watched her sad eyes turn in his direction and saw her mouth form silent words, "Help me."

Her pleading look chilled him in spite of the poaching suit's temperature control.

He checked the sky, tabbed the safety back on, and picked his way along the boulders to the edge of the kill zone. He paused at the clearing. The hapless woman lifted her arms in a silent plea. She said something he couldn't make out.

"Run!" he yelled. "Get away from the tree!"

She twisted in the grip of the tree, but she couldn't

pull away.

"Stupid tree-hugger," he said. If she had a permit, no one would look for her until it expired. By then, the tree would be finished with her.

He'd have to find another tree. He didn't want to get mixed up in a death.

"Help me." Her voice was weak on the breeze. She leaned away from her captor, reached for him.

"Shit," he said, then he headed across the kill zone, fast and careful, one eye scanning the sky for bots and one scanning the ground for roots and pinecones. "Stay still! Don't move!" he called. If he was lucky, he could cut her loose and get to cover before the skybot made another pass. One thing was sure, grandma Sitka would stand tall for at least one more day.

Picking his way across the last three meters of sun-dried needles and dust, he found himself staring. The woman's cheeks glowed opalescent white. Her eyes were wide and sad and full of the lonely darkness of a cold mountain night. Her arms rose and opened to him. He stopped, almost close enough to touch her. He balanced the sawmill on his hip, one finger on the trigger guard and one on the safety.

She whispered, "Help me." Her whisper carried on a breeze of sweet breath. "Help me."

Sweet breath. He stepped closer, inhaling the scent of her. His stomach warmed. His fear of tree and sky dissolved. He slipped his free hand around her narrow waist.

"I'll help you," he said. "It's okay, I'm here."

Strong, lithe arms welcomed him. Lips as cool and soft as dew-laden moss rose to meet his. The kiss was long, her tongue honey sweet and wise.

She rocked him slowly in an embrace so tight with need that he thought she might never let go.

He pulled away for breath. Her eyes widened. Her grip tightened. She whispered, "Help me."

Dieter pressed his free hand between them to lever her away.

From her shoulder, a third arm sprouted, and a fourth. A hand grew from her belly, ripped through her tattered shirt, and wrapped itself around his crotch.

Dieter screamed. He tried to bring the sawmill to bear on the tree trunk behind her. One of her new-grown hands crushed his hand and his mill.

He screamed again. He bit her shoulder. Bitter Sitka sap filled his mouth.

"Help me," she whispered again. "Help me." Over and over, her drugged breath washed over his cheek.

Dieter struggled until her embrace became so tight he could only move his head. Finally, he went limp, resting in an embrace he knew would tighten, knowing he was a dead man, knowing his grandfather had tried to warn him.

He should have known. The alarms never went off. He should have listened. Should have waited a day or two.

For long hours, he waited for his end in the Sitka's embrace. Shadows became longer until the sun fell away to the west and the night's first down-slope gust chilled him.

Still, death did not come. Her whisper softened to the sound of needles rustling above his head, and he began to fear the patience of a tree. She needn't crush. She had covered him from sight with her many arms. He could barely move. His hand was pulp, his sawmill crushed. She could wait for thirst or hunger or cold to kill him. The silence of waiting was in her heart.

Dieter twisted his head. By the silver light of a half moon, he could see the broken remains of his father's sawmill lying in needles and dust. Shadowy carpenter ants explored the twisted mill. He wondered if the ants were ecotech, if they liked meat and how long it would take them to find him. Already, he thought he felt their tickle inside the legs of his suit.

A chill rose from his bowels. He shook in the embrace of the tree. Pride led him to this death as surely as it made his father forget the alarms.

He glanced at the star-clad sky. A shadow passed in the distance. Instinctively, he checked his suit temperature. He laughed at himself. What did that matter now? He was dead anyway. No point in fearing skybots. He pulled his head back into his hood and tried to pinch the suit's thermo control between his tongue and one of the tree's many arms.

He pressed, sweated, and twisted. Finally, he felt the click of the tab under his tongue. The suit flushed hot. He hoped the skybot could get a thermal image through the woody arms surrounding him.

As Dieter waited in the darkness, the tickling on his

legs became certainty and grew into a maddening fear. Cold, thirst, and hunger became deaths he would welcome as his pounding heart marked off endless minutes. Anything would be better than the slow devouring of the ants.

Just as despair closed his heart in darkness, the skybot attacked. Heat and white light exploded around him.

A tickling on his cheek woke Dieter to cold morning light.

Ants!

He rolled and slapped at his face. Pain exploded in his cheek. His face was badly burned where neither the Sitka's woody arms nor his suit had protected him from the skybot's blast. He braced his hand against the ground, attempting to get up. A second explosion of pain from his shattered hand dropped him back to the dust. He held it before him. His trigger and safety fingers were crushed and useless.

Dieter fought to slow his breath, to get the pain under control. Shaking and nauseous, he struggled to his feet. Holding his damaged hand against his chest, he reset his temperature control then faced the tree. One side of the trunk was scorched, but the bark was thick and the tree wasn't really hurt. At his feet, a mass of charred wood still smoldered, tangled branches still reaching toward him. The woman-shaped bait was no longer recognizable in that mess.

Dieter slowly stumbled back from the tree.

Where he had stood, the ground parted. Dark hair and the top of a head sprouted. Dieter fell back. He scrambled backward through the dust.

A new copy of the woman rose from the earth in all her unblemished glory.

Her arms came up. Her sad eyes opened. She whispered, "Help me."

He turned his head to avoid her sweet breath. Finally, he whispered the word, "No."

She pointed at the charred remains of her earlier self. "Please."

Dieter wanted to run, but he was weak and hurt. Her breath reached him and pulled at his heart. He tried not to breathe in, not to hear, not to care. Even so, he looked where she pointed.

The skybot's blast had burned open a great root. Carpenter ants, normal carpenter ants, swarmed within, trying to put their nest right, a nest that was slowly eating away the life of the Sitka.

Dieter stood and ran.

Franz waited at the cabin door, axe in hand. When Dieter saw the old man's scarred face, relief became shame. Blood rushed to his burned cheeks, and his face screamed with new pain.

Dieter faced his grandfather. The old man hefted his axe, his two-fingered hand gripping it beneath the broad blade.

Dieter reached out and saw his own tangled fingers. "Trigger and safety," he said.

Grandpa Franz nodded. "Her breath is sweet, eh, Dieter?"

"How long?" Dieter asked.

"Our war ended before you were born."

Dieter took the axe. "You prune with this?"

Franz nodded. "How is she?"

"Ants have her in a bad way," Dieter said. In spite of the pain of his burned face, he smiled, then turned toward the woods.

"She'll give you everything you need, Dieter," Franz called after him, "if you let her give it instead of tryin' to take it."

Dieter nodded, then slipped into the cool shadows among the ferns and rhododendrons beneath the trees.

Last of Our Kind

by Heather S. Ransom

Burnt and bloodied, my heart raced faster than my legs. I sprinted after the other women, down the long, dark, briny tunnel. Our heavy breathing and unsteady footfall; the only sounds I heard beyond the pounding of the blood rushing through my skull. Darkness pushed in at every angle, threatening to steal the others if I fell too far behind.

Focus. Do you want to lose them? To be alone ... here?

The logical part of my brain demanded attentiveness. An alertness necessitated by survival. But another part battled for an awareness of the improbability of our situation. And, with it, a new weariness seeped into my already exhausted body.

This doesn't make sense. This can't actually be happening. Not here. Not now. Not like this –

"It's not much further. Hurry. We can't afford to slow down. We're close." A curt female voice, rough, edgy.

The taller one ... is she the research development scientist or the naval engineer? I couldn't remember.

Think, my brain insisted. *She's the one who–*

Abruptly, the woman in front of me stopped, causing me to step to the side of her and smack my shoulder into a slick wall. Turning to say something, I hesitated, seeing a door that one of the other women was unlocking.

"Liz, hurry."

"I am. Stay back. It's stuck or something. I–"

A sharp clicking sound interrupted her sentence, and she jerked it open.

I felt a presence next to me before I recognized the dark figure. Zeva.

"I don't like this," she whispered in my ear. "I'm not sure I believe them. I mean, we don't really know for sure what's happening out there." I felt the tension in her voice, and couldn't say I didn't share the concern. But my logical side kicked back in.

"We need to–"

A hand on my shoulder caused me to hesitate and turn.

Shae's voice, gruff, shaky. "How could this–"

"This way. Move. I'm locking this door behind us. We have to get to the next one quickly." Another voice. Or was it the one from before? I couldn't remember. I needed to slow down, to stop, to think....

We moved through the door. I glanced back behind me, where I thought Shae would be. But I couldn't tell if she was there. With the door closed, this new area was even darker. I opened my mouth to say more, but then we were once again moving at a speed that forced me to focus on my footing, leaving no opportunity to speak.

Less than an hour ago, I'd been laughing, talking, enjoying coffee and cookies with my friends. It already seemed like a different lifetime.

My mind flashed back to earlier in the day. The First Annual National Women's STEM Symposium. A nation-wide event that had brought together the most brilliant female minds in science, technology, engineering, and mathematics: the leading scientists, mathematicians, computer programmers, physicians, research analysts ... and teachers of STEM subjects in schools across the country. Thousands of women with these incredible minds, gathered in twenty cities across our nation. Same day, corresponding times. All with one focus. How we, as women, could set the example for our daughters, for the next generation of females: fierce intelligence, confident enthusiasm, overwhelming passion. Over five million women. We would change the world.

My school district had sent all of us – state and federal monies had covered the cost. We were ecstatic to be chosen to attend. Twenty-six secondary female educators. Science, math, technology, and technical careers teachers. I'd volunteered to complete the application.

Had it just been yesterday that we'd all flown in together? Checked into our hotel? Drank a glass of wine, sharing what only women can share when they celebrate their common bond?

"Keep close. This section splits off multiple times. We don't want to lose any of you." The curt voice again.

I stumbled slightly. Regained my footing quickly. *Focus. This isn't the time to reminisce.* My logical side working to take back control.

"You okay?" Amina's voice, just in front of me. Concerned, she must have heard the stagger in my steps.

"Fine. Keep going." My voice sounded so assured. So confident. So certain that we were doing the right thing. After all, they were only here because of me. Because I had talked them into taking a "little side venture" with me. I always knew what I was doing ... shit, what had I gotten us into?

Talking them into "sneaking out" with me hadn't been difficult. I mean, I had proposed an hour or two away from the conference, a few miles down the road, just enough time to check out a book signing at a small local bookstore, and then back to the conference. No one would ever know we were gone. We would arrive back just before the big presentation, the one where the twenty women from each of the conference locations would all simultaneously be on the big screens as one panel, speaking to the work that women could do, and *needed to do*, in our country today. It would be about our contributions, our steps, our leadership.

Zeva had been all in. Books were her thing. Shae and Amina had also agreed, ready to take a break from the intensity of conference classes. Mifawny joined at the last minute. I had our route planned out. It felt a bit like

"Mission Impossible," sneaking past conference attendants, down deserted hallways, through a back door of the enormous stadium. Then, it was just us. Laughing, walking, joking, commenting on the beauty of the night.

As promised, the signing ended on time. With a wink, I told my friends we might even have a minute to buy a drink on our way back. Zeva pursed her lips, reminding us we needed to be back for the presentation. That it was what we were really here for. We each took out our conference identification lanyards, putting them back on. The party would have to be postponed.

But it never happened.

As we waited for our ride to arrive, a massive explosion rocked the world around us. One second we were laughing and talking, the next we were lying haphazardly on the ground, strewn like paper dolls caught up by the wind. I sat up first, ears ringing, black spots floating through my vision. Slowly, I identified the others. Mifawny had blood trickling down her face from somewhere in her hairline. Shae was checking on Amina, the two huddled close together. Zeva's eyes caught mine with a bewildered look. For a moment, we simply stayed like that.

Then the sirens and lights broke through into my clouded mind.

"What the hell just happened?" Zeva said, standing shakily, leaning to help Mifawny up.

"Oh, my god." It was Shae's voice. I turned.

It was gone.

The immense stadium full of all those incredible

female minds: my friends, my colleagues, my heroes. Those we had left behind... all gone.

Suddenly, there were people everywhere. We pushed back toward the stadium on foot. Together but silent. Looking for those we knew in our hearts we wouldn't find. From time to time our eyes locked, but the words never came. So, we simply pressed on.

About a half mile from the stadium, we were stopped. Barricades were already being set up. Emergency personnel looking for "survivors."

I felt my throat catch as I stared past an officer. There weren't going to be any survivors. It was utter devastation. If I hadn't tasted the ash, smelled the smoke, and felt the heat, I would have thought it was a scene from a movie. Something like this didn't happen here. It had to be a movie.

Funny how our brains try rationalizing the irrational.

"... *not just here. Haven't you heard? All twenty locations were attacked at the same time.*"

"... *Middle Eastern terrorist group. My guess is al-Qaeda.*"

"... *Taliban group taking credit. Millions are dead.*"

"... *just heard on the news that Al-Shabaab is possibly involved.*"

Everyone around me was talking. Pieces of the discussions registered in my mind as I continued to stare at the destruction in front of me. The five of us moved closer together.

"I just spoke to a news reporter from Channel 5. All twenty locations of the women's symposium were bombed. At the same time. Everyone is saying it was a coordinated terrorist attack." Zeva's voice was low.

I stepped in closer. "All of them?"

Amina bent over, the pain on her face obvious. Shae hadn't moved.

"Are there survivors?" The blood on Mifawny's face had dried leaving a jagged red line down her cheek. No one answered.

They each turned back to look without speaking. I didn't need to look again. I knew. I wanted to close my eyes - to remember what it had been like before... to discover this was just a dream. That must have been it. I was sleeping. Dreaming. A nightmare I needed to awaken from.

A hand caught my arm. Then came a voice I didn't recognize. I opened my eyes, instantly returning to my reality.

"You were at the Women's Symposium?" Hard eyes looked at the badge hanging from my lanyard to those worn by my friends as well. A man in a military uniform. I nodded.

"The other women at the conference? Do you know if–" My voice broke.

He threw up a hand to cut me off mid-sentence. "Please, woman, pull yourself together. We need all of you to come with us. We're trying to make sense of this. Follow me." His hand remained firmly attached to my arm, but his eyes darted towards something in the distance.

Pull yourself together? Woman? I shook off his hand,

ignoring his glare. "Who are you? Why–"

"Did you hear me?" He pulled himself up to his full height, towering over me, chest puffed out. Roughly, he grabbed my arm once again.

Wrong move, asshole. Even as I drew a breath to tell him off, Shae was there. In his face. "Take your hands off her!" Her voice was loud enough to draw the attention of the crowd around us.

The officer stepped back, throwing his hands up. "Ladies, please. We're gathering all of the symposium attendees we can to help identify survivors. Many are badly wounded. We need your help."

Shae stepped back and looked to me. Survivors?

In unspoken agreement, we fell in step with the officer as he hurried us away from the crowd. "Wait here," he said, leaving us near a military transport vehicle, as he moved toward another officer just up the road with a larger group of women.

The conversation seemed animated. Women pointing and yelling. Something wasn't right. I felt it in my gut.

Whispers behind me caught my attention. I turned around to see Zeva talking in hushed tones with a woman I didn't know. Mifawny moved toward them and after a few seconds looked up at me, mouthing, "Come on." She turned with Zeva and followed the woman. Shae and Amina motioned rapidly for me. What had I missed?

One more look back then I, too, was headed away from the road, down an alley, into the darkness. "Zeva?" my voice a harsh whisper. Why was I whispering? What in the hell was happening?

A shout rang out from behind us. Then another. Then the sound of running.

Then, we were running. Why were we running? Zeva's quick glance back cut short my questioning.

Fear. In her eyes. I'd never seen her like this before. I just kept running.

At some point we slowed, but we never walked. The way the others kept looking behind us imparted an unrelenting urgency. There were sporadic introductions; intermittent directions. I couldn't quite catch up with Zeva to find out what was going on but her intensity to keep moving was unquestionable, so we followed.

We were getting closer to the ocean, the salty air burning the back of my throat. We entered an old warehouse, moved cautiously to the rear of the building, down a flight of stairs, and into a basement area. Finally, we paused.

"Zeva." I grabbed her arm, pulling her closer to me. "What is going on? Why are we following them? Where are we?"

"Something's really wrong out there. I met Liz earlier today at one of my workshops. She's into some interesting research development with viruses and–"

An alarm went off in the building, like a fire drill at school, unreasonably loud and shrill. My hands flew to cover my ears.

A door was open at the other side of the room. A woman was yelling at us, frantically waving her arms for us to follow her into a dark, narrow tunnel.

We were all running again. Time seemed lost here. The darkness stole any perception of normalcy. Then we were at another door. It was all I could do to try to catch my breath. I wasn't sure I could run any more. I wanted answers but I couldn't form the words yet.

The door flew open and light flooded the tunnel. Blinded, I felt hands pulling me forward, bodies herding together. Then, everyone was talking all at once. Questions. Demands. Directions. But no one was listening.

Someone whistled.

The woman who seemed to be in charge held up her hand. Prompt silence.

It was then that I took a moment to look around this brightly lit area. Now that my eyes had fully adjusted, I could see what looked like a high-tech facility. Computers, monitors, lab equipment. Some sort of underground... lab? Bunker? Or... I'd never seen anything like it. Except in the movies - sci fi movies. Or war movies....

"... naval research facility. We're getting out of here now."

I snapped back. What had she said? Naval facility? She was military? What? My mind was playing with justifications again, trying to piece together the information, to come up with a plausible situation....

I jumped as a large, roll-up, metal door began to rattle open. A partially underwater cave appeared in front of us. Three vehicles sat on what looked like metal slides.

"Who's driven a motorcycle before? Or a

snowmobile?"

I had when I was a kid. Growing up in the country, we'd had both, but that had been a long time ago. Could I still?

"I have." It was Shae.

"Me, too." Mifawny stepped up beside her.

Then we were all at the vehicles. They looked like a cross between some sort of science fiction submersible and a multi-rider snowmobile, but enclosed with a clear, domed top.

"... like a motorcycle. Lean forward. Stay forward. Keep the accelerator locked down. Watch the compass and go north. Stay at about thirty feet – there on the dash, it's a depth reader." Mifawny and Shae were nodding their heads, listening intently to the woman who had led us here.

"Everyone get in. Three in each. We have to get out of here now!" No one asked questions. Everyone started climbing over the sides. Amina started to follow Shae into one of the vehicles. Shae stopped her, saying something about separating, so that if anything happened to one of them, the other could take care of their boys. A quick, tight hug then Amina was behind me. Mifawny was already in the front of our vehicle looking at the panel.

Wait. This was happening too fast. We needed to stop to talk. *Where are we going? Why do we have to leave now?* My mind spun as it searched for information that I hoped I had heard. I'd already come this far.

My body wasn't listening to my brain. Even as I was thinking that I shouldn't be getting in, I found myself squeezing in behind Mifawny and then Amina behind me. The three of us seated but leaning forward *hard*. Zeva was in the next vehicle over. She was right behind Shae, Liz behind her.

Finally, I found my voice, and tried to stand. "Are you sure we need to do this? What about the others? Can the terrorists get us down here? I mean, the Taliban, or whoever's responsible, they're not going to know about this place, right? I mean–"

"What? What do you... wait, you don't know? It's not some terrorist group from another country who's just killed all of those women." It was the Naval woman. She stood at the front of the third vehicle, staring incredulously at me. "Five million of the brightest minds in our country were just eliminated, but not by terrorists. It was our government. Our *own* government orchestrated the attacks. Those officers up there weren't taking you to identify survivors. They were going to finish the job. There weren't supposed to be any survivors. Period."

My mouth opened but nothing came out.

"We don't have time to do this right now. Stay if you want, but we're leaving. They will be here any minute. They'll know I'm here. We used my access card to get in." She stepped over the side into the third vehicle, checking the readings on the dash.

"But why?" I couldn't wrap my mind around this. Not my country, my government, my–

"Where have you been? Haven't you been following the news? Watching what's been happening to women across the country? The way we've been treated? Disregarded? Shamed? Laughed at? Looked down on? Really?"

"I – I – I, I mean, it's not that bad, is it? I mean...."

She shook her head as she continued, "It was perfect. All of us, determined, smart, strong women. They found a way to gather us together, with the promise of a chance to change the world. We were all so eager for it to be true that we jumped at the proposal. It was like sheep to the slaughter. They planned to take us all out at once, hoping the ones left would be afraid, easier to control. I'm sure the media is already telling women to stay indoors – hide behind the protection of the men around them and to watch for more 'inevitable' terrorist attacks against women–"

Sirens cut off her ranting. All eyes flew to the rolling door behind us.

"There's no more time. We have to go. This may be our only chance to get out. Follow me the best you can. Ride hard, as fast as possible for about forty minutes. By then we should be past the border. I have friends up there. They'll help us."

Amina pulled me down into my seat. The clear dome closed over us. Leaning forward, I clutched Mifawny. I could feel her heartbeat with my cheek on her back, could feel Amina clinging to me.

In the next second, we were racing through the water. For a brief moment, I could see Zeva's face looking at me. Then she was gone.

We were all gone.

In the Days of El Dorado

by Joanna Michal Hoyt

"No, Marisol," Esele says, trying to sound calm while half-shouting. The heavy shutters over the windows only slightly diminish the scream of wind and lash of waves. Maybe the noise seems worse because Esele and the children shut into this floor with her can't see what's going on out there, can't help imagining it. "No, we can't look out now. The wind and rain would get in."

"Then I want to go up where the windows are uncovered," Marisol says.

That's the next floor up, where Esperanza (Marisol's mama) and six other grown-ups watch over the Arkipelago as the hurricane sweeps by. Esele and the kids, Esperanza and the grownups, are in one of the two buildings that still has its feet on dry ground; the other solid-rooted tower is on another island a quarter mile away. The tower buildings between and around those islands go down into the water; food gardens grow on their roofs, but it's not safe to go inside them, because they might come crashing down in storms like this one.

That's what the little kids are told. Esele understands no place is safe in the storms, and that's why Esperanza is watching: If one of the three arks full of gardens and people and animals founders, or if the other solid island gets flooded by the surge and its tower starts to come down, Esperanza and the people with her will have to decide if they should send the boat chain out to rescue people or if that would just make them lose more people and boats, which is why Esele and the kids can't be with them.

"No!" Esele says. "You heard your mama. They have to look, and decide what to do, and do it. We have to stay out of the way."

"But I could help them!"

Esele is thinking much the same thing. She's twelve. She was out with the grown-ups all the day before, harvesting what they could (not much, so early in the season) from the tower-roof gardens and the arks, helping to bind some of the floating junk together into barriers which might stop bigger junk from plowing into either. Her arms and her back still hurt from that, but if they launch a rescue...

Then the kids should be safe inside. It's Esele's job to keep the kids where they're supposed to be. Also to launch their lifeboat and get the kids all into it if this tower starts shaking. Also to feed the rabbits on the floor below if the grown-ups all go rescuing and don't come back.

She is not going to have to do any of that, she tells herself. She wants to help, but not that badly. She shakes her head at Marisol, and at herself.

"You helped yesterday. We all did. Now we just have to wait. Come on, get some more water for *los chiquitos*."

"We just had water at lunch."

"This storm's filled the cisterns again, so we have plenty. Anyway, if our throats are all dry, how can we tell stories?"

"Stories?" Marisol asks, sounding a little calmer.

"Anything you want—just nothing really spooky that would scare *los chiquitos*. Come on, all of you, sit close so I don't have to yell."

Marisol seems mollified by the fact that she, at ten, is not being counted among the little ones. She pours water, holds the cup while Miguelito drinks. Eufrasia is starting to shake again, so Marisol sits down behind her, starts working on her braids, her hands slow and steady. Esele watches a moment to make sure Eufrasia is settled, then asks them all, "You ready for a story?"

"Yes!" they chorus.

"Tell about the Golden Age!" Marisol calls.

Esele sits cross-legged and spreads her hands. The little ones quiet, waiting for her to begin.

"Long, long ago," Esele says, "the Arkipelago was part of the Big Island way-away out there." She points north-by-northwest, through another shuttered window, toward the tower from which, on a clear day, you can just see the Big Island on the horizon. "And the tower islands weren't islands at all. They were on dry ground. Nobody needed boats because the people could get everywhere on land. You could start from the ocean on one side and walk every day for a year and still not reach the ocean on the other side."

Some of the little ones look wondering, others doubtful.

"There was food everywhere. They didn't have rooftop gardens on the towers, because they had all that dry land to grow on. And in the water there were lots and lots of fish, real solid fish you could eat, not jellyfish, and none of them were poison."

"So they all had everything they wanted," Eufrasia says, wide-eyed.

"No, they didn't," Marisol says.

"Well, everything they needed," Eufrasia amends.

"No, they didn't," Esele says. "Not all of them. Because—does anyone know why?"

"Because of the gold," Marisol says.

"That's right," Esele says. "In the Golden Age in *America*—that's what they called the Big Island then, *America*—you had to have gold before you could use anything else. There might be food growing out of the ground next to you, or sitting on a shelf next to you, but you couldn't take it unless you gave a person who had lots of gold some of your gold. If you didn't have any gold you had to wait until somebody who had gold agreed to give stuff to you. Mostly the people with gold gave the no-gold people just enough food so they didn't die, but not all they wanted."

"Like hungry-year rations," Marisol says. Four years ago the storms wrecked most of the crop and everyone ate just enough to stay alive. Marisol was old enough to understand and remember.

"Hungry-year rations for people who didn't have gold, and lots of everything for people who did," Esele says.

"Why didn't people just take food anyway? Was the gold magic?" Eufrasia asks.

"Sort of magic," says Esele, who has never understood this part. "And you needed gold for everything, not just food. Back then, when people got sick, they could cure it fast and certain, sure—there were special things to eat and drink that killed the sickness right away."

"Like Concepcion's herbs."

"But they worked faster, and they almost always worked. And sometimes they could just give you something like a mosquito bite, but instead of putting the sickness into your blood, it took it back out. But you had to give gold for that, too, if you wanted a really good cure. If you didn't have any gold the people with gold would fix some kinds of sickness, 'cept you had to wait longer and it didn't work as well."

"Where did the people get the gold from?" Reuben wants to know.

"Sometimes they got it out of the ground," Esele says. "But there was just a little bit of it in the ground, and it was hard to find. Sometimes they dug up big pieces of the ground and burned them in a special fire that turned the dirt into gold, but it took a lot of dirt to make a tiny little bit of gold. They had to burn the dirt slowly and just a little at a time, because the burning made the air hot and the smoke made people sick if they breathed it, and in the holes where they dug the ground out there was slime that made people sick if they touched it."

"Yucky!" says Miguelito.

"And if you put big piles of gold together they grew even bigger all on their own," Esele adds.

"How?" Marisol asks.

"Sort of by magic," Esele says, and hurries on before Marisol can ask for an explanation Esele can't give. "But mostly people got gold from other people. People with no gold could do work for people with gold and get gold, a little, little at a time. People with lots of gold took gold from other people for food and sick cures and stuff, or they fought each other to get more, or they tricked each other for it."

"Like the Gold Sacks Man who made the houses crash," Marisol says.

"Huh?" says Eufrasia.

Esele nods. "The Gold Sacks Man told everyone that he'd learned a new way to make gold grow fast-fast if you put enough of it together. Lots of people believed him. They put their gold in sacks and took it to him, and he locked it in a special room and said special words over it. He said it would take a whole month to grow, so people couldn't take their gold back out until the time was over, but they could look in through the windows and see their sacks swelling up and getting bigger and bigger. So they were happy."

Eufrasia is smiling. She hasn't heard this story before.

"So on the ending day the Gold Sacks Man opened up the doors and everyone ran in to get their sacks. But he said, don't open them here, take them home first, or maybe people will steal your gold. So they ran back to their houses and shut the windows and locked the doors and went up into the upstairs rooms and they opened their sacks."

"And they were happy," says Eufrasia.

"And they were not happy," corrects Esele. "Because what they saw in the tops of the sacks wasn't gold. It was rocks. Rough funny-colored rocks that were still swelling and growing. So the people dumped the rocks out, thinking maybe the gold was underneath. But there wasn't any gold anywhere in the sacks, just those rocks, and the rocks grew so fast in the air that they were huge boulders when they hit the house floors, and the houses fell down with a great big CRASH." Esele shouts the last sentence, hoping to cover the sound of feet clanging down the outside stairs. Someone must be putting out a rescue boat.

Eufrasia starts to shake again. "Were the people dead?" she asks in a small tight voice. She's just old enough to remember when one of the tower islands collapsed and two of the gardeners drowned. One of them was Eufrasia's cousin.

"No," Esele says, more to reassure Eufrasia than because she's sure it's true. "No, but they didn't have houses any more, and they didn't have gold to get new houses with..."

"Couldn't they make their own houses?"

"They weren't supposed to make anything if they didn't have gold."

"Cause of the magic," says Eufrasia, apparently satisfied with that explanation. "But where had their gold gone?"

"Nobody ever knew," Esele explains. "It just disappeared, and so did the Gold Sacks Man. So the people were angry and scared and they wanted more gold again, and they wanted it fast. Some people said they should try putting up the houses again without gold and letting people live in them so they weren't sleeping outside in the cold rain. But other people said the houses wouldn't be real unless people put gold in for them, that they'd fall down again, so they needed to get more gold to make the houses real."

"How could they get more gold?" Eufrasia asks. "Did they go to find the Gold Sacks Man?"

"They tried," Esele says, "but nobody ever found him. So they were angry and they felt stupid, and they argued about whose fault it was. They kept arguing until El Dorado came."

Esele reaches in her mind for the words Aunt Selma used for this part of the story, tries to make her voice swing and ring like that.

"El Dorado had a lot of gold that he hadn't given to the Gold Sacks Man. His hair and his face were the color of gold, and he lived in a giant tower made of gold, and the light in there was like the most beautiful sunset you ever saw, all day, every day."

"Did he give people gold from his tower to build houses?" Eufrasia wants to know. "Or did he take them to live in his tower with him?"

"No, he said all that gold was his, but he said if everybody did what he said, they could all have their own gold towers," Esele says. "So they all promised to obey him. And they gave him another house to be in while he was bossing people around, a great big house as white as children's teeth."

"Why did they give him that house," Reuben wants to know, "if he already had a big tower house and a lot of people didn't have any houses?"

"Because he had gold and the no-house people didn't and that's how they did things in the Golden Age," Esele says. "And because they thought if they gave him stuff and made him happy then he'd make more gold so everybody could have nice houses. So they gave the white house to him, and he stood in front of that house and told everybody what to do. He said they had to change the rules that made them go slow and careful when they were burning ground into gold. He said if people burned ground into gold as fast as they could there'd be enough gold for everybody. At least, for everybody who was good. He said there were too many bad people on the Big Island, and if they were all gone then there'd be more gold for the good ones."

"But how did he know which ones were good?" Eufrasia asks.

"Good people were gold people," Esele says. "Gold-hair people, and people with lots of gold stored up, and also people who liked El Dorado and all his gold. He said no more people could come to the Big Island unless they were gold people, and he sent away some of the not-gold people who'd come from way-away, from other big islands."

"Did they go to the Arkipelago?"

"No, 'cause there wasn't any Arkipelago yet, this was still part of the Flower State in *America*, and he was sending people out from here too. He sent people back to the big islands they came from. Even if there wasn't any room for them there or any food. But he couldn't send away the not-gold people who were born in *America*, so he tried to make them be good or disappear. He said not to give any more food rations or sick cures for people without gold in their sacks, cause that just made there be more and more bad not-gold people. If everybody had to give gold for everything then soon there would only be good gold people left."

"But what happened to the people who didn't get any food?" Eufrasia asks.

"What do you think?" Marisol rejoins. Esele hurries on.

"Then the Big Sick started. People got sick faster-faster-faster and it was really hard to fix them. Some people said the not-gold people got sick because they weren't getting any more cures or because they were too hungry or because there was more smoke in the air from burning up the ground. But El Dorado said the not-gold people were dirty and mean and made sickness on purpose. So he sent more of them away. But some of the good gold people got sick too, and they paid all their gold for sick cures, and they were still sick, so then they turned into bad people and they didn't get any more help. So all the good people were afraid of turning into bad people."

"They must have been really scared," Eufrasia says.

"Yes, they were. Scared and angry. Some of them even got angry at El Dorado. But he told them they'd all be all right if they burned the ground even faster; if they obeyed him and burned very fast it would bring back the gold and make them all good again. He stood in front of his white house and said that, and the sun shone on his golden hair, and they believed him. So they kept digging up the ground and burning it, faster-faster-faster."

"Did it work?" Reuben wants to know.

"Part of it," Esele says. "They made more and more and more and more gold, and soon other people were building beautiful gold towers like El Dorado's. But some people still didn't have any houses. They didn't even have places to put houses on cause the ground had gotten dug up and there were just holes full of slime left. So the no-gold people lived all piled up in the shadows of the gold towers and they were mad, mad, mad. And the people inside the towers were afraid of the people outside. And the people outside threw things at the people inside whenever they had to go out, and they tried to break the tower walls, and the people inside dropped things out of their windows on the people outside, and the fighting got worse and worse."

The little kids look scared now, their faces gray and drawn in the grudging light of the storm lamp. Probably she shouldn't have told them this story. At least she can leave out the scarier bits of what Aunt Selma has told her. She will skip the stories of the Big Fight and give the easiest version of the ending that she knows.

"And God looked down, and he saw how the people were hurting each other," she says. "And he saw how the earth was all getting burned up. And he started to cry. God's tears filled up the oceans and made them come up, up, up. God's tears fell in the holes where they'd dug up the ground and burned it, and those places filled with water too. The ocean came roaring in over El Dorado's gold tower and it fell down CRASH."

"Was the Golden Man in his tower? Did he die?" Reuben asks.

"He got away. He ran up-up-up into the Big Island. But after his gold tower fell down people didn't do what he said any more. They looked at his gold hair and his golden face and they thought about his smashed gold tower and they just turned away and put their hands over their ears when he tried to talk to them. And they saw the ocean coming up-up-up and they decided they didn't need gold after all; they needed land."

"That was smarter," Reuben says.

"So they stopped fighting?" Eufrasia asks.

"Not all of them," Esele says. "A lot of people saw there wasn't going to be so much land as before, and they wanted what was left for themselves, so they tried to push other people off into the water. The people who had lived in the gold towers said the land was theirs cause they were good, and the people who had lived in the shadows said the land was theirs cause the gold people had already turned their share of the land into gold and slime and the rest of the land belonged to the other people." She looks at Eufrasia, who sits very still with stricken eyes, and sends her what she hopes is a reassuring smile. "But some of the people who didn't have much gold decided not to fight and not to use gold or make slime. They made gardens on the roofs of the tower islands that had their feet in the water, and they raised rabbits and they caught fish, and they ate what they grew and caught without paying any gold for it, and it still filled them up. When they got sick they took care of each other. They lived in towers on the little islands, and they made arks out on the water for people and animals and plants so there was room for everyone. They built the arks without any gold, but mostly the arks didn't sink after Nora got the pontoons right. And they had children, and their children had children, and those children had children, and here we are today."

"Here we are," Miguelito repeats, smiling. Marisol nods.

"That's not how my Dat tells the story," Reuben says. "He says soon the gold people were the only ones left on the Big Island, and they kept making more gold so the gold magic would stop the salt water coming up. They burned everything up to make gold until there was nothing left, no food and no fresh water, just gold. So they died. He says there's no people on the Big Island now."

"But what about their children?" Eufrasia wants to know.

Esele doesn't want to answer that.

"Somebody's still there," Marisol says. "Or they used to be. Mama says when my Bisabuela Asunción was a little girl and some of the hollow islands got drowned, people from here took a boat to the Big Island to see if there was room, but people on the Big Island shot at the boats, so the boats came back, and it was after that Nora built the arks so there would be room for all of us here."

"They're just stories," Esele says before Marisol and Reuben can start arguing. "We don't know for sure what happened on Big Island after our people stayed in the Arkipelago. Maybe the Big Islanders started to take care of each other too."

Footsteps come up the outside stairs. *Please please please*, Esele thinks, *don't let anybody be dead.*

The stairs door opens. Esperanza comes through it with Eufrasia's ma Manoo leaning on her. Manoo was on the ark with Reuben's father Ezra and some other grown-ups, and with the egg chickens and the bean and pumpkin plants; now she's soaking wet and limping. Esperanza's wet too—she must have been on the rescue boat.

"Where's Dat?" Reuben asks, his voice shaky.

"He's alive," Manoo says. "Everyone's alive." She stops to cough up salt water. Eufrasia gets her a towel and a bowl. "We're all alive. Reuben, your Dat's sick from swallowing salt water, but he's breathing fine, he'll be alright. Esperanza and Ibrahim pulled him out of the water and now Concepción's getting all the water out of him. We'll row you over to Amadou and Concepción's ark to see him."

"And your ark...?"

"Broke up. Pulled the anchors, hit one of the garden

islands. We lost a lot of the egg birds and all the plants. But the storm's blown over now, we're all alive, we'll be alright. And the other two arks are fine-fine."

She doesn't say that it will be another hungry winter. Esele understands that.

"But why are there still floods?" Reuben wants to know. "We don't do gold, we're helping each other. It isn't fair."

"Mama says nothing's fair," Marisol says in a flat dead voice.

"Right now I say it's fine and fair that we're all alive," Esperanza says. "And it's beautiful... Come on up, come see."

They hurry up the stairs after her, look out the open window holes. Towers of clouds sail east and away, the sunset light flaring on their undersides. Out to the east, the other island's tower still stands, and the ragged silhouettes of two arks bob on the water. Southaways the tower islands are a dark grid against the bright water. Westaways the last two garden islands, Manoo's ark, and everything that grew on them have disappeared, swallowed by a vast expanse of tumbling gold.

Fantasia for Gun Control:

Tiresias, Songbirds, & the NRA

by Stephen Scott Whitaker

Dress in three kinds of plaid to cross
three different lands, to be
of three minds on Sunday,
to be three in the morning, wise
at nine.

Challenge, challenge, challenge go birds, because
it's spring. Because
they have no guns
they sing. Because they have
no guns, birds riddle.

*Ai me, Ai me O, come
for me.* A trill,

a push
of air. Wings
snap, cut
up, push
up, break
from limb,
tree rattle, ah----sh,
ah----sh,
ah tuh, ah tuh
ah--sh, ah---sh.

Dress in three plaids to cross three
different lands, to be of three minds
in the afternoon to be three
in the morning, wise at nine.

Mine! My,
me eye, oh
to do, to do,
to do

Money pulls the trigger, money
shakes the trees. It is spider
ichor, a money trigger.
Egg sacs lay in pockets
everywhere. Only birds
are to be trusted

with truth. A dash of glamor,

a pin for a jacket, skip
at the sound. To do, to do
to do. Mine, mine,
mine. Remember
the dead. Birdsong floats.

Challenge, challenge, challenge:
Hibiscus, hibiscus,
A rattle of cedars.
Hi yay, hi ho, hi yum.
You are small, small, small.

Emma's Knives

by Karen Eisenbrey

(An earlier version of "Emma's Knives" was included in the anthology *Ted Cruz Smiles and a Baby Dies*, Pankhearst, 2016)

Dear Emma,

Some would have you believe there's only one good way to make chicken soup. Nonsense. There are as many ways as there are cooks. Here is the method I learned from my grandmother. Over the years, I made it my own. Feel free to do the same.

Invest in a good stockpot. Don't rely on roommates or partners to provide cookware.

Acquire the best knives you can afford. Don't be afraid to use your knives. Keep them sharp.

1. *Roast a chicken, free-range if possible. Freedom improves the flavor.*
2. *Carve off wings, drumsticks, thighs, and breast meat. Serve immediately or set aside for another meal. Leave back meat on carcass.*
3. *Place carcass and juices in stockpot.*

4. *Add vegetables. My recipe calls for chunks of carrot and celery in equal amounts, and sliced onion. It is possible to make a satisfying soup with onion and only carrot or only celery if that is your preference. The amount of onion is up to you, but if you will be sharing the soup, it is helpful to agree.*

5. *Add water to cover, put lid on pot, and place over high heat until boiling. Skim foam or stir it down.*

6. *Reduce heat, replace lid, and simmer for a few hours. Taste periodically. Trust your senses. You'll know when it's ready!*

7. *Strain bones and vegetables and allow stock to cool. (Compost bones and veggies, if possible. It's important to give back to the earth.) Chill to allow fat to harden for easy removal, or leave it in if you like; it's your soup. Use in recipes that call for broth or stock, including:*

GRANDMA'S CHICKEN SOUP

Chop half an onion (more or less as you prefer). Heat 1 tablespoon oil in a large pan and sauté onion until translucent and yielding. Add diced carrots and/or celery (see above), one cup each if using both. Sauté, stirring occasionally, 5 minutes. Meanwhile, cut up some of that leftover chicken; mix light and dark meat for fullest flavor. Add 8 cups stock (if strong, dilute with water) and chicken. Bring to a boil. Taste and season according to your preference. Soup may be served as is, or add your favorite noodles or dumplings. Recipes available upon request!

Good soup is not complicated, but can take years to master. I hope you find it a worthwhile challenge, and that you find someone to eat it with you who shares your taste in onions. Invest in a good stockpot. Keep your knives sharp.

Love, Grandma

Emma waited for the light, anxious to get out of the sun and out of sight. Traffic — and traffic laws — didn't favor pedestrians. The same people who could afford private vehicles made the laws, or controlled those who did. Jaywalkers didn't stand a chance. It was every man for himself, and heaven help a woman on her own. According to Grandma, she needed to be ready and able to help herself. Make her own soup.

In theory, it was safe to be out. Active fighting had abated to the occasional insurgent uprising, usually in some remote place. Law-abiding citizens with nothing to hide had nothing to worry about. In theory.

Emma gazed up at the tower of the old church across the street. Highrise apartments dwarfed the once grand edifice. Emma didn't know if they even held services there anymore. That brand of Christianity had long fallen out of favor with the regime.

Would the signal never change? Emma's parents claimed to remember when summers weren't so hot, storms so powerful. Grandma scoffed and said things were better than that when she was young. Emma doubted she'd fondly recall these sweltering days — unless it got worse.

Her long sundress would have been perfect for the weather ... except for the high-necked, long-sleeved blouse she wore under it, tucked into jeans, tucked into boots. She'd already sweated through everything. She adjusted her sunglasses and wide-brimmed hat, wishing she could wear short sleeves, like the men at the bus stop in front of the church. Some women did; there wasn't a dress code. Just a Byzantine collection of unwritten rules that "everybody" knew, although you didn't really know them until you'd broken one.

Was that guy staring at her? She felt self-conscious of her bare hands, but she drew the line at gloves in summer.

The light changed. Emma hurried across and around the church building to the lower level entrance. She tried the door — locked. The directory listed a food pantry, a counseling office, a low-income clinic, and something called Free Range North. Nothing like what she was looking for. But she'd come so far. She pressed the buzzer.

"Who do you seek?"

"Abby?" Emma answered as she'd been instructed.

"Third door on the left."

Clunk. Emma pressed the handle and the door opened. So far, her information was good, but she still didn't know what it meant. She passed the doors for the social service agencies listed on the directory. The sign on the third door read Free Range North -- Accurate Bookkeeping, Notary Public. She counted again to be sure, then knocked.

A little panel slid back. "Who's there?" A man's voice, gruff. Nothing like an Abby.

"I'm Emma."

"Well?"

Emma hoped she remembered the correct phrase. "I have ... a gift for Abby."

The panel slid closed. Interview over. Then the door opened. "Inside, quickly."

Emma stepped through. The man was tall, dark, and younger than he sounded. He leaned out and looked up and down the hallway before closing the door. "Did anyone see you?"

"I don't think so." The cramped office was little larger than a broom closet. "Why are you here?"

"Accurate bookkeeping, notary public."

"Uh huh."

"Or did you mean why are we in the basement of a decommissioned church? The rent's affordable and many of our clients are here."

"But why would a bookkeeper need a password and the whole speakeasy routine?"

"All good questions." He sat behind the desk. "Please, sit."

Emma took the chair across from him. If it was a trap, she hadn't yet said anything that could be held against her. To be safe, she slipped a small knife out of her boot and held it in her lap.

"Smart," the man said. "You won't need it here, but smart."

"I keep my knives sharp." Emma didn't care if he understood. She found her grandmother's phrase reassuring. Homely cooking advice, and more.

He nodded once, a respectful bow. "Well, since you asked — this is a legitimate bookkeeping firm, for the agencies in the building and a few other clients. And for those with the key, a connection to ... something more."

"You're not Abby."

"No, I'm Gabe. Abby's the key."

"I don't believe you."

Gabe smiled. Emma could believe he'd been a student not long ago. "Have you heard of the girl who blew herself up and started the rebellion?"

"My grandmother told me the story." Not her parents. They wanted nothing to do with either side. "That was Abby?"

"She was just a girl, years younger than either of us. I don't know exactly why she did it, but it's clear she'd had it with the powers-that-be."

Emma could relate, even if she didn't plan to blow herself up. Maybe she'd come to the right place, after all.

Gabe's expression turned serious. "If I answer your question about why I'm here, will that help you trust us?"

"It might."

He sat back, gazed at the ceiling, inhaled and exhaled a long breath. "When I was nineteen, I saw my best friend beaten to death by a mob for the crime of holding hands with his boyfriend in public."

"Wow. I'm sorry." Emma had heard similar stories, but not from anyone this close to it. "That isn't even a crime."

"And apparently neither is murder when committed in the name of religious liberty. The killers were charged with disturbing the peace."

"Shit." Women weren't supposed to swear — more unwritten rules — but the word slipped out before Emma could stop it.

"Yeah. I'd guess you have your own story along those lines, or you wouldn't be here."

"Nothing quite as violent as that. Or maybe it is." She sighed. "I was brought up to believe if I worked hard and didn't make trouble, I'd be a valued member of society. But that was a lie. I can't be trusted to make my own decisions, and I was only valued for something I can no longer do."

"It's a harsh place to be a woman."

"We can be harsh right back." She gripped the knife handle. "I raised some money and I want the rebels to have it. I didn't know where to transfer the funds, so it's in cash." Emma pulled a cashbox out of her bag. She released the clasps and lifted the top.

Gabe stared. "This isn't a gift. It's ... an endowment! Where did it come from?"

"Long story."

"I'm not going anywhere."

"Short version: it came from a Wal-Mart voucher."

Gabe whistled. "Maybe my question should be 'how' rather than 'where.'"

"I have ... good investment instincts."

"You don't look like a stockbroker."

She started to smile, then caught herself. "I'm an intern." She wanted to trust Gabe. She didn't even know him, but already she liked him. She didn't have a lot of carrots in her soup these days, and no onions at all.

"An intern."

"You know, get coffee, maintain social media sites, keep your ears open and your mouth shut? Intern."

"At a brokerage? You must have learned plenty. Are they going to hire you permanently?"

"I got the internship so they could show how fair everything is — women aren't restricted in education or hiring. But they wouldn't want to take a chance on someone who's just going to get married and have babies and drop out of the workforce within the next five years. Right? Not their fault women are like that." Something Emma had overheard while keeping her mouth shut. She wasn't about to tell her boss no man would marry a woman who couldn't have children. It wasn't his business, and it might give him ideas.

"Their loss. I still don't get the part about the voucher."

"It was ... compensation. For something I ..." Emma's throat closed around the last word. *Lost*? No. Something that was taken — stolen. Something of hers they decided she didn't deserve.

Emma had been born at a moment when her parents had paid off their student loans, were both working, and finally had decent insurance. Things went steeply downhill almost immediately — not their fault, but the best they could do was keep their heads down, avoid attention, stay out of trouble, and not get fired.

Emma's own troubles began when she was twenty-one, a full-time student amassing debt of her own. Her fling with Zayden wasn't love, but definitely *like*, with potential for more. He was smart and passionate, they were young, it was summer ... Then something failed and she had a bun in the oven. No, more like a spaetzle. Her lack of insurance didn't matter. An unmarried woman couldn't get coverage for contraception or maternity care. And she couldn't have married Zayden if she'd wanted to. By then, he was gone.

Everything seemed designed to make her feel bad about her decision, though the procedure was legal. The anonymous clinic at the industrial edge of a mixed-use zone, housed in a cheap building like the portable classrooms outside an over-enrolled elementary school. The multiple-choice questionnaire with answers that didn't quite fit, with no "none-of-the-above" options. The smug counselor ...

"Do you have any questions?"

"Where is the restroom?" The only non-sarcastic remark Emma could think of.

Counselor Kathy directed her down the hall. Emma hoped to find her period had started and she wouldn't need any services, but no such luck. She looked at herself in the mirror. She could walk away, figure something out. But there wasn't anything else.

"Better?" Kathy's smile didn't reach her eyes.

"Much. So what else do you need to know?"

"You've said you don't plan to marry the father of your child. Does he know ...?"

"No. He died at Snipe's Mountain."

Kathy clucked sympathetically. "We lost a lot of good soldiers there."

Emma nodded. Zayden hadn't told her what he planned to do there, but he wasn't active-duty military. She could easily imagine which side he'd fought on. "I simply can't be pregnant now. They'll kick me out of school if I don't drop out, and I'm nearly finished — one more semester."

"Have you considered adoption? We're connected to a very good home. They have classes right there, and you'd be kept busy until time to deliver. Your baby would go to wonderful, deserving parents."

Emma wanted to scream. Did she look like a high-school girl? "I'm finishing up a business degree. Then I have an internship, and then I need to find work so I can start paying back my loans."

"I see. What are your goals?"

"I'd like to work in banking or finance if I can — use my skills and training to support myself, help other people with their money issues." *Use my knives. Keep them sharp.*

"What about marriage and family?"

"That's not really a goal." Emma would welcome a family at the right time, but it wasn't something she could make happen alone. "I can't be pregnant right now. It doesn't matter who parents the baby, because this baby ... can't be. I'm already eight weeks along. I need to take care of it now."

Kathy folded her hands on the tabletop. "If you decide to go that route, I'll go over some educational materials with you, so you know all the details of your baby's development and possible harm to your mental and physical health. Then there's a three-day waiting period. So many girls in your situation change their minds when they realize they'll regret it for the rest of their lives. But if you decide to go ahead, the basic termination procedure can be performed for only $1000."

Emma gulped. That was a lot for her, but she could come up with it somehow. Grandma might lend it to her, or maybe they had an installment plan ...

"... but we would have to add your name to a national database."

So much for her dream of any kind of decent career. Employers always did a background check. "Isn't there any way —?"

"I'm getting to that. With the deluxe package, your records are handled with the utmost confidentiality."

"And how much —?"

"Only $10,000. But ... there is another option. An experimental procedure, but we've had good outcomes."

"What kind of procedure? And how much?"

"There's no cost to you, and you'll benefit a deserving Christian couple desperate to bear a child. Think of it as adoption, but you don't have to be pregnant."

"How?"

"It's a kind of ... transplant. Someone else has the joy of carrying your baby to term. Since there's no termination, you remain anonymous, and the couple will pay for the procedure. It is delicate and time-consuming, but you'll get medical care, transportation, even compensation for your trouble."

It was too good to be true, but once Emma had read the brochure, it sounded like the answer to everything. "Alright. I'll do it."

There was no mandatory waiting period. Kathy led Emma through a hidden door and down a staircase to a gleaming medical facility, completely at odds with the aboveground appearance of the clinic.

"We'll admit you now and perform a few tests to make sure you're a good candidate, then match you with a prospective mother. We happen to have a few ladies on site today, so if all goes well, the transplant will be performed tomorrow."

Emma was too dazed to answer. Tomorrow was Friday. She didn't have classes on Friday, so that was all right. By Monday, she'd be her old self again.

The next morning, a doctor visited her room to explain the procedure and have her sign releases. She was given something "to relax her," so she didn't understand half of what he said, but signed anyway. The next thing she knew, she was waking up in the recovery room, her brain still foggy. She tried to sit up and moaned at the intense pain.

A nurse rushed to her bedside. "Don't try to get up yet. You'll tear your sutures."

"Sutures?"

"From the surgery."

"*Surgery?*" There was a word no one had used before. The nurse lifted Emma's gown to check something. A sutured incision cut across her abdomen like a smile — or a frown, from her angle.

"Why ...?"

"Don't you remember? You've had a hysterectomy. Your womb was transplanted into a woman who deserves to bear a child."

"But no one said ... I never ..."

The nurse flicked through her chart. "Is this your signature?"

It was. Emma read something about the "embryo/fetus and its surroundings." Nowhere did it say *hysterectomy*. She'd heard of uterine transplants in cases where the prospective mother didn't have one of her own, an extreme and nearly miraculous form of fertility treatment. But the donor was usually a relative, or deceased. And the uterus wasn't occupied until after.

"What if I wasn't done with it?"

"You told your counselor you had no plans for marriage or family."

"No, I said it wasn't a goal!"

"Well, perhaps someday you'll be worthy of a transplant yourself. In the meantime, you need to learn how to care for your incision while it heals."

They discharged her the next day, wheeling her through a maze of hallways to an exit that was not the way she'd entered. Unlike the small clinic designed for maximum shame, the state-of-the-art fertility clinic was all about making patients feel virtuous and hopeful. Yet the two were connected underground by an experimental procedure. Emma didn't feel any ill will toward the other woman. She hoped the pregnancy would succeed and the family would be happy. Emma's loss wasn't their fault. But it wasn't hers, either.

Emma left the facility in a cab someone else had paid for (transportation) with a paper sack of pain meds, antibiotics, and a sheet of post-op instructions (medical care), and a $7500 Wal-Mart voucher (compensation). She considered tearing it up, but her good financial sense got in the way. It had value, even if she decided not to spend it herself.

Still in the cab, she sent an urgent text to her grandmother: *I need you.* The reply arrived before she had unlocked her apartment door: *on my way.* Grandma arrived ninety minutes later, with groceries. Emma reclined on the couch and spilled her tale while Grandma filled the studio apartment with the healing aromas of comfort food.

"$7500 would buy a lot of necessities."

"If I spend it on myself, they've won. Maybe I could barter it for legal services and sue that clinic."

"It does sound like they're preying on vulnerable women, at both ends of the deal. But even if you find an attorney who'll take that trade, a case like this could turn nasty for you, and there's no guarantee you'll win. And if you do, does that restore your womb, or any other options?"

Emma considered that. She might win a monetary award. The clinic might be thoroughly investigated, or even shut down. But the root cause would remain. "You're right. The real bad guy is a regime that doesn't regard women as adults who can make their own decisions. That's who I should go after."

"You want to sue the government?"

"I want to take them down."

Emma took a week off from school, claiming an emergency appendectomy. A classmate kept her up to date on assignments. She'd have to creep back to school before she was fully recovered, but Grandma promised to stay as long as she was needed. With that lifeline to hold,

Emma started trawling barter sites. She didn't want to trade for $7500 worth of something else. She wanted to find someone who needed the voucher more than they needed what they had, even if it was more valuable.

A young widow had inherited her grandparents' furniture. The woman had no space for it, and couldn't afford the storage fees, let alone an appraisal. Her children's need for food and diapers outweighed any sentimental attachment to heirlooms.

Emma contacted her with an offer of the voucher. When they met the next day at a coffee shop to make the handoff, the mother wept with gratitude and handed over the code to the storage unit.

"There's antiques in there, probably worth a small fortune, but I just can't deal with it right now. Or ever. You're doing me a favor taking them off my hands."

The storage unit was full of solid, well made pieces — tables, chairs, beds, bureaus, armoires, a glass-fronted china cabinet — all in immaculate condition. And in one drawer, Emma found a case full of vintage jewelry. Back on the barter site, she found an appraiser who would value everything for a percentage. After he took a selection of the jewels, Emma traded the rest for a classic car that needed work, with enough left over to secure the services of a good mechanic who was down on his luck. The car went in trade for a dilapidated condo, which Emma flipped for adequate funds to start day-trading.

By this time, she had begun her internship. She heeded her boss's investment advice, though it wasn't meant for her. Between that and her own instincts — and tax laws that favored investment income — she amassed a small fortune in short order. She set up a trust fund for herself — she still had those loans to pay off — but the rest was for the rebels.

"We're lucky our leaders underestimate the abilities of women," Gabe said when Emma had finished her tale. "We'll have to launder the cash through fundraisers, but then we can reinvest it and make use of the earnings. Any restrictions?"

"No guns or bombs."

"How do you feel about propaganda? Winning hearts and minds? Or food and medical supplies are always needed."

"Those would be fine." Emma slid the knife back into her boot and stood.

"May I ask one more thing before you go?"

"Sure, what?"

"Now that we have an endowment, we'll need someone to manage it."

Emma smiled. "I thought you'd never ask."

Dear Emma,

I'm so happy you want the dumpling recipe, too. Small luxuries improve even the best soup. These are rich, but not doughy. The recipe doubles or halves readily, so make them for yourself alone, for you and friend(s), or for an army. This one goes way back, to the 30 Years War.

GRANDMA'S DUMPLINGS
1 cup milk (substitute water in hard times or for lighter dumplings)
½ cup butter, margarine, or chicken fat
½ cup flour
4 eggs

While soup is heating, place milk and butter in a saucepan over medium heat and bring to a boil. Remove from heat and let stand for a few seconds. Add flour all at once and stir until dough pulls away from pan. Let cool slightly. Add eggs one at a time, beating after each addition until smooth.

Dip a soup spoon into boiling soup (this allows the dumpling to release). Scoop up a spoonful of dumpling dough and drop it into the soup. Dip the spoon again and repeat until all dough is used. Cover soup pot and reduce heat to low. Simmer 10 minutes. Dumplings will puff up, so be sure your soup pot has enough room.

(Secret: A different cooking method transforms the same dough into dessert. Bake spoonfuls at 400° F for 30 minutes. When cool, cut open, hollow out, and fill with whipped cream, pudding, or ice cream. Cream puffs! Because even in wartime — especially in wartime — we deserve something sweet.)

The Runner

by Meagan Johanson

Please be here, Jin thought, ducking low as a fire-tipped arrow whistled over her head. Someone was hunting Unsworn tonight. She only had a second to look.

The black pond spread before her, purple fireflies beginning their constellate, one by one. This was where Jin would find him, if anywhere. He would bring her here, on the rare late night afforded by their parents, to watch the fireflies come to life. The cool air on her skin. The crickets singing. This was real magic, to little Jin.

But that was before the Northern border closed. Before the scavenge, the fleeing. Before much of the southern soil had turned to sand.

It had been 127 days since Jin had last seen Theo. And he wasn't here now - in this realm, at this moment.

Fingertip fast, she opened a new vision window and checked off the server from her list.

Realm: Naishre (Guerrilla)
August 6, 2102
22:30:07 AST

Mirror Pond

62 realms down, 8 to go.

Counting days. Notching minutes. Pressing a thick black line through something. Jin hoped to find her brother here, but the game was more than that to her. It was evidence of some small power. It was measure and meter, something she could hold.

A fresh rain of arrows peppered the ground at her feet, and she leapt away from the green circles left behind. The violence was worse than normal tonight, even for a Guerrilla realm, Sun- and Shadowsworn out for the hunt.

Jin could run. The dark embrace of the Naishre forest stretched behind the pond. The forest turned any player stealth, but was filled with thirsty black unicorns and soul ravens, not to mention real-life players waiting to net runner geolocations for real government reward.

No. The forest was not an option.

Inside the Witch's Well, she could safely port away, but the inn would be filled with players of all ilks and eyes; Naishre was notorious for its black market dealings - runner-capture just one of many. A single long-scan from a geared bounty hunter and her sister and Grandma, all the runners scattered in District 9, would be exposed. And they wouldn't even know it until the border police knocked on their doors.

A single arrow lodged hard into a great moaning oak behind Jin. Her decision was made. She dashed from the pond towards the inn, and plunged right in to the heat and din, the last-ditch sanctuary, of The Witch's Well.

Immediately, Jin began her port, knowing the entire room would see the glow of her spell, her immediacy. But she needed to get out fast. As the spell began, she glanced around the common room. Scantily clad skins, the usual raucous emotes.

Two strangers from the back noticed Jin, her glow. One pointed, while the other, a silver-skin, stepped out of the crowd. His eyes turned black, chin lowered, and he began to scan her. The first player switched forms to a cat and dashed across the room to her. With a huge paw, he pinned Jin's neck against the thick wall of the inn.

She should have cast haste first. The port spell was too slow. She wasn't going to make it out. Everything was too tight, too close. She couldn't breathe.

"What's your hurry, girl?" he hissed at her, then sniffed. "A runner. I can smell the stink on you." The silver-skin was next to them then, scanning her point blank in earnest. He didn't take his dark eyes off her.

"You don't know me." Jin wiggled under the pressing claws digging in to her skin. Five, six, seven. She felt seven claws.

"Refugee, then. One and the same, showing up where you don't belong."

"Prefer only places where water still flows, fat boy? I bet you've never even stepped foot in the south."

The player switched to human form, tall and wide, still holding her neck, but now with an armored elbow that nearly crushed her windpipe. "Of course not. I don't step where the shit is. You done scanning yet, Ovi?" he asked over his shoulder.

"A few more seconds," the silver-skin answered, forked tongue slipping out between words.

Fury and fear pounded inside Jin's chest, and she struggled back and forth, trying to catch the eye of anyone for help, even though Jin knew this wasn't a crowd to break up a fight.

"Keep her still," said the silver skin.

She wasn't going to escape in time. The port wasn't complete. She would expose everyone and still no Theo. No message, no footprint.

Jin closed her eyes hard, as the tears began...

... and as a fresh burst of pain shook her body.

"What are you doing, Jin?!" an angry voice spoke in her ear.

A familiar voice.

Jin removed her blindfold, opened her eyes.

She was back in her small bedroom, in bed, the warm liquid of her haptic blanket quickly cooling, shrinking around her. Her older sister, Ellis, loomed over her.

"I saw your realm. Get up, before I punch your other arm." With a ripping zip, her sister yanked open the haptic bag, deflating it in full.

"Careful," Jin said.

"Grandma is sleeping. Otherwise I'd be yelling at you. Guerrilla realms? Really? Just because you are fourteen now does not mean you get to do whatever you want, go wherever you want."

"Go wherever I want? You're funny." Jin sat up slowly and rubbed her neck, the phantom grip lingering. Her mouth was dry, golden hair a knotted tumble. She'd been in the game for over an hour, flipping through realms.

Ellis paced back and forth once across the room, her tall, thin frame lost in her bulky nightgown, her own blonde hair swept into a loose bun. Then she sat down on the edge of the bed, slipped her hand into Jin's. "You can't keep looking for him, Jin. You are going to get us thrown into the cages or sent back home. Think about Grandma."

"He's your brother too, you know." Jin said.

She didn't tell her sister that capture was mere seconds away, or that Ellis saved her by disconnecting.

"I miss him, too. And Mom, Dad. But our home and our family are here now. We have to protect what we have." She gave Jin's hand a squeeze, as if the conversation was over.

"What if Theo is trying to find me in there too? He doesn't know where we are. All I need is a few seconds to pass him a message, a dark code, something only he would...."

"No!" Ellis shot up from the bed, grabbing the bag. "This is not some quest you can try again tomorrow. If you fail it could mean life or death, Jin. There's no restart. I sometimes forget that you are still a little girl, with little thoughts." She let a long breath leave her body, then spoke softer. "We have another long day tomorrow in the meathouse, and your algebra test, too. You should get some sleep."

With that, Ellis clicked off Jin's lamp and stepped out of the room, taking the blanket with her.

Jin flopped back in the darkness to the still warm bed.

On the ceiling, the streetlamp made an elongated shape of white, perfect lines where the light met the dark. Parameters.

If only everything was so easily defined.

"I want my blanket back," Jin said, spooning a cool mouthful of food into her mouth. Grandma's egg salad - her favorite. Plus two blackberry jam cookies. "I won't go to any of the dangerous realms, I promise."

"Someone has to take care of you, Jin. Someone has to be the mother."

"*Mother* would want us to find Theo. Do you have any better ideas?"

Ellis shook her head. "Work hard and keep your head down - that's what Grandma would say."

Jin slid away from Ellis's side, pulling her thin shirt off her neck in billows to cool her skin. It was always summer inside the meathouses, but especially in the cafeteria. It smelled like a tropical bbq - old seaweed, salted pork. Except the pork wasn't pig. Not anymore. It was a hybrid plant, Ploink™, grown for its thick, pink leaves of meat-like sponge. Instead of grain and grass, it fed on slurries of algae and minerals. And sunlight, of course, which there was plenty of up North. Actual animal meat was extremely expensive now and much of it illegal to have or eat.

Ellis took another bite of salad, eyes scanning the

entrances, exits. There were hundreds of meathouses north of the border. The fact that illegals, underage or otherwise, made up the majority of their labor force was no secret. Lucky for Jin and her sister, northern white collars enjoyed their Ploink™ immensely and most chose to look the other way, rather than bend down any day of the week, even on a Sunday. But the trembling possibility of a runner crackdown was always there, humming low under the skin.

Each worker was given a close-to-expiry plant every Friday at day's end. Between Jin, her sister, and Grandma's cooking, two plants stretched their protein for an entire week. Ground, spiced, fried - it tasted almost as good as an old-fashioned sausage.

Almost.

"What does your Grandma note say today?" Ellis asked.

Jin pulled out a small, yellow, wobble-scripted note from her lunch sack. "'Always take the scenic route.' What about yours?"

"'Heart is where the home is'," Ellis read.

"Close enough," said Jin, opening her pouch of cookies.

Ellis's eyebrows lifted playfully. "I'm thinking today we do something crazy. Wild. Unexpected."

"Pretend we are sick and go home?" Jin asked.

"You know we can't do that. I was thinking... instead of Math Monday, we pretend it's Science Saturday." Ellis pulled out a heavy, battered textbook titled BIOLOGY.

"Hmmm. I do like Science Saturdays, almost as much

as Story Sundays." In truth, she enjoyed all her studies with Ellis, even Finance Fridays. Getting lost in that focus, roaming in thought; there weren't many places left to do that - roam.

Jin cracked open the textbook, spine long broken. "I know where it is, you know. My blanket. It's in the hall closet, rolled up behind the jackets. Seems a good place to store it, actually." She bit off a piece of cookie, the jam sweet in her mouth. Dessert first seemed the good kind of sin.

Ellis stuck out her tongue at Jin and for a moment appeared a young girl herself, instead of a matronly 22. Then she took a bite out of her own cookie, blackberry jam sticking to her upper lip as she talked. "Page 266. Eat your salad."

Jin found the haptic blanket folded neatly on her bed when she went upstairs that evening. She unfolded it and slipped inside, the liquid already expanding around her, conforming to the weight and heat of her body, amplifying. Remembering the promise to her sister - knowing Ellis *was* right - Jin logged in.

Realm: Beltran
August 8, 2102
21:22:35 AST
Mirror Pond

Realm after realm, the pond unfolded in her vision with each jump. Dark and smooth, the pond was the constant, living up to its name. A mirror.

When Jin started playing the game years ago, she chose Unsworn, just like her brother had. Only two years older than her, Jin looked up to him.

"I'm sworn to no one," he explained. "Not the light or the dark, sun or shadow. I'm the in-between. I belong to no one but myself. And neither should you, Jinny."

Self-possession.

What a wonderful safety in those words. Something she longed for still. A room of her own. Four walls to hold her, but with a wide open ceiling of sky.

When Jin, Ellis and Grandma left, Theo didn't hug her goodbye. They were granted asylum in the north before the government stopped accepting refugees and the border was sealed. Theo had to stay behind with her father, in case the Army called. Her mother chose to stay. Jin had Ellis to take care of her. And Grandma.

"I'll see you again, Jinny," he had said. "No need for goodbyes."

That was 129 days ago. She was angry at him, then. But her anger smoothed to sadness now. And Jin would give up all of the jam cookies in the world to feel that hug.

At 10:30 pm, the fireflies came, one by one, glints over the water. But no Theo. No breath, no heartbeat, no rhythm. No pattern in the static.

Jin stepped to the edge of the pond. The smooth surface was alight with violet sparks reflecting. She pulled out her weapon - a long sword glowing a low blue flame along its blade. *Better than nothing*, Jin thought, and leaned over the edge of the water, holding the blue light close to her face.

She was in one of Theo's skins. He had given Jin mimic access to his appearances long ago. This one, his main look, was a tall, broad-shouldered human, in cartoonish similarity to his real-life likeness. Dark hair, dark eyes, pale skin, their father's genes. It was almost him, this ghost she carried. This in-between.

"I belong to no one," she whispered to the water.

Then Jin began to cry. And her reflection cried right back.

What I Miss Most:

1. *Theo*
2. *Mom*
3. *Dad*
4. *Mz. Mittenz*
5. *Honey*
6. *Hamburgers*
7. *Fourth of July*
8. *Snow*
9. *School*
10.

"Do you have lunch in your bag?" Jin asked, swinging her leg over the long table bench, arm rummaging elbow deep. The last hurray of August's end had transformed the meathouse cafeteria into a bog of stink. Jin was looking forward to fall, and smelling something besides sweat and ferment.

She turned her pack upside down over the table and emptied its contents out. Her study notebook, a pen, and a handful of Grandma's crumpled blessings tumbled out. But no lunch.

Ellis furrowed her brow, quickly searched through her own pack, then shook her head. "I thought my bag felt light this morning. That's not like Grandma." Jin could hear the sink of worry in her sister's voice. "I've got a little pocket cash. I'll go get us something from the machines."

Jin pulled her long hair up off her neck and waited, counting the notes from Grandma in front of her, two by two.

Ellis returned with grape popsicles, and Jin tore into the package, grateful for the cool sweetness. Popsicles melting faster than they could eat them, the sisters ate in silence, wondering what they would find returning home that night.

'That's not like Grandma," Ellis repeated, pulling out Jin's textbooks with her free hand.

When the popsicle was gone, Jin gathered all the

notes up, carefully flattened them up, and put them back in her bag. There were 42.

"She's not here," Ellis said, returning to the kitchen from the back room where Grandma slept. "Her bed isn't made. She never leaves her bed unmade." Ellis's voice wobbled, eyes darted.

"The lunches were made, and in the fridge," Jin said, then passed Ellis one of the notes Grandma had left inside.

"'Have the sunrise and this bloom make the days all home,'" Ellis said, crumpling up the paper.

"Maybe she's at the market with Isobel?" Jin asked.

Ellis shook her head. "I called Izzy. She hasn't seen Grandma since Tuesday."

Jin's eyes lit up. "We can track her! With the chip. Everyone with that disease has one, right? Dementia."

Ellis's voice was far away. "She took it out, Jin."

"Took it out?" Jin was horrified. She tugged out a few of the soft blonde hairs on her arm.

"It didn't hurt. It was in the cartilage, under her hair. Dad helped her remove it right after the implant. The stitches were fresh, skin still numb. Jin, if Grandma had the implant, they'd know where we are. She had to take it out. Dad has it back home."

Jin looked down at the dining table, at the wavy wood grain. A fan hummed in the window, moving the summer evening's heat around the room like warm tongues on their skin. Outside, a child's voice called the name of a pet to come inside for the night.

"I thought you said this was our home," Jin said under her breath.

"It is." Ellis looked up at her, a resolution solidifying in her gaze. "Let's go find her."

It took 23 minutes to find Grandma, in the thick of the alders along the lip of Skunk Creek. She had slept the whole night on the sandy bank, huddled inside Jin's haptic blanket, or what was left of it. The fabric was torn and flat, gel drained and sensory feathers scattered to the wind.

Grandma waited all night for the bus, but it never came.

It was a good thing she had her jacket.

"Once upon a time there lived - "

"A fairytale?" interrupted Jin with a groan. "Story Sunday has taken a turn for the cliché."

"I never said it was a fairytale," Ellis responded. "It might be a dystopian horror. Nothing scarier than real life. True story."

"If it's a fairytale you want, I have a good one," Grandma said, winding some yarn from an old sweater into a ball. She was making a new blanket for Jin. Not quite the same as her shredded haptic one, but Jin was grateful for the sentiment. She had started saving nibbles from her paycheck each week for a new gaming bag, but it would be winter by the time she could afford it. At least she'd be warm.

"The stage is all yours," said Ellis, laying back on their sagging floral couch, sweeping her legs up and into Jin's lap.

"This is a love story," Grandma said, her two needles beginning their weave. "It was 2042, summertime in Connecticut, the hottest on record. The storms hadn't yet blown away the topsoil. Plants still grew, animals still roamed. Ticks had been finally been eradicated and ADAR1 gene therapy perfected. It was a year on fire in so many ways. The boy and the girl met in medical school, even though she would like to say it was on the balmy Long Island shoreline rather than General Orthopedics rotation. The girl would like to say the boy stumbled into her, interrupting a good beach read with a careless football toss. Perhaps he tripped on her towel, and both of them laughed through the tussle. Perhaps by the end of it, she ruffled the white sand out of his thick, dark hair. Maybe he kissed at least nine of her freckles and touched a lock of her red hair. Was she part-Irish? Yes, Dear Reader, she was."

Ellis winked up at Jin. Both sisters had heard this story before, but each new version was never quite the same, by accident or design.

"The girl fancied herself a vintage kind of feminine," Grandma continued. "Aprons and lipstick, 20th century modern modest. She hoped to find someone to care for with an old-fashioned swoon. A boy to fawn over and to be her world, even if only in pretend. She was a strong woman. Of course she was. The boy would need to be worthy of her woo." Grandma paused, as a wet cough shook her small frame. When it was finished, she shook her head. "Love stories certainly are silly, aren't they?"

"No love story is silly if it's true," Jin said.

"Oh, it's true." Her body started back up again then, chair rocking, needles clicking, words coming out quick fire. "Well, your grandfather wouldn't let me dote on him like I wanted. He took over all the ministering, the cooking and cleaning. Do you know he used to pack my lunch every day? And he'd leave me a little note inside, every time. I still have some of them, pressed into my Doctor Zhivago. And we did go to Long Island a few times, even though swimming was prohibited by then due to the red bloom. He bought me cream sodas while we walked on the sand. That was happily ever after enough, in my book."

Grandma's needles stopped their dance, yarn hanging motionless next to her boney ankles. Then she slowly got up, setting her knitting aside.

"Well, if no one is going to tell us a story, I'll make us a snack. There's some fresh olives and crackers I got with Izzy today. Would you girls like a snack?"

Jin kept her eyes on Ellis. "We'd love some,

Grandma."

What I Miss Most:

1. _Theo_
2. _Mom_
3. _Dad_
4. _Mz. Mittenz_
5. _Honey_
6. _Hamburgers_
7. _Fourth of July_
8. _Snow_
9. _School_
10. _New York_

"You can borrow it as long as you like."

James's voice cracked when he spoke. He ran a nervous splay of fingers through his sandy hair. Once. Twice. His eyes were the color of a winter sky with no clouds in it. Was this love?

"Are you sure?" Jin asked, pulling the bag to her chest. It smelled like James: soap and sweat and the vanilla candles his mom was always burning in their kitchen.

"I'm sure. My dad gets them discounted in Quebec

when he travels. We have three."

Yes, this must be love.

A flower pressing roots down the center of Jin, a mouth of velvet petals.

A compass pointing north.

Gravity.

It only took 263 heartbeats to walk home.

Realm: Tzsuul
September 22, 2102
22:29:47 AST
Mirror Pond

The pond was still there. Dark glass and crickets. Fireflies shaking out of the virtual ether.

Jin knew now she would not find her brother here, at a single moment out of all the realms with endless waypoints. She knew her search was a downy thistle seed, a copper coin - a little girl's wish.

The first step in to the cold water took her breath away. Slowly, she eased in, the cool lapping at her ankles, legs, waist. With each step down, the black swallowed more of her body. She could see nothing below the surface, only darkness reflecting. Would she disappear as well, under the molten black?

She inhaled one, two, three deep breaths, then sunk under the surface, down down down to the smooth floor of the pond.

She was inside the reflection now. Contained. Held.

Above her, the purple fireflies shimmered, shivering moonlight behind them. From here, the violet flecks hovered in a single plain, a different view. She noticed something she hadn't seen before, from above.

A pattern.

Words.

Had they been here the whole time?

Jin's heartbeat flooded her ears with sound.

She couldn't breathe.

Spelled out in tiny purple sparks, clear as day, right above her, was the message:

On my way

Jin tore off her blindfold and opened her eyes.

"On my way," she whispered into the cool dark of her room. She sat up, unzipped the bag, threw her legs off the bed. Across her wall and ceiling, the long white light of the streetlight spread, just as it always did.

She went to the window and opened it, her skin bristling with goosebumps at the night air. The maples were just beginning to change, red to orange to yellow. The north still had seasons. Jin looked down the quiet street at the quiet houses filled with quiet beds. How many people lived on this road? How many colors and shapes of them, wishes big and small? Too many to count.

This was her world now. Her home.

District 9, Newfoundland, Canada

"On my way."

Jin said it again through a wide smile, but this time, all she could hear was hope.

The Creamy Ichor Sauce Over Lake Michigan

by TJ Berg

Many have asked that I write an account of the events that led to our current state of affairs. My involvement was only peripheral, but my association with the university during the time that the events unfolded has left my name with a touch of notoriety. And so I'll leave this document, a testament of what I witnessed, for those still able to comprehend it.

My first professorship was at Miskatonic University, at which I thought to make a name for myself in the ancient linguistic arts, decoding the guttural words of the heathens whose strange sounds were the precursors to our now sophisticated languages. I will not detail the horrors that faced me on my first field research expedition--the dread that had crept into that clean, quaint town. Their failed ritual. Suffice it to say, when I fled the cursed hills of that north-eastern town with its inky harbor and slinking milky horrors that called themselves people, I thought a sabbatical on the shores of Lake Michigan would bring me peace. I suppose it did, though not in the way I thought it would.

The Wisconsin lakeshore was not what I expected. It is hard to imagine, if you have not visited, the expanse of Lake Michigan, its steely gray waters melting into the horizon, the fury of its white caps in a storm ... and the people. I expected Wisconsin to be filled with friendly, unsophisticated people who enjoyed beer and sausage a little too much. I thought there would be cheese. A lot of cheese. There was. A lot of cheese. They bread it and fry it and dip it in creamy sauces.

The sauces. The sauces like ichor coating a crisp, greasy savory bite of cheese curd. It was one of the offerings those friendly, unsophisticated people made, during that dark night of unspeakable horror. I am too far ahead of myself. I had found a house swap on the coast, where I had planned on doing some writing and research in quiet solitude. The owner had left a booklet with things that might interest me. Local events. Wholesome things, like the county fairs.

Should I curse the moment I decided that the tinkling bright lights of a fairgrounds would lift the dark fingers from my soul?

This one was set up on the coast and smelled of hay and manure, fried food and cotton candy, and beneath it the oozing wet smells of unhealthy algae coating the shoreline. And the people, all kinds of them, like some great horrific mix of all the peoples of the earth. I saw a woman in one of those things Muslims wear, a hijab, eating cotton candy with her cantering child. There were so many kinds of people I almost wished to be returned to that quaint north-eastern town with its pale, milky folk. I had not thought Wisconsin would be like this.

But the funnel cake had called to me by then, clasped my mind in its crispy, sweet tentacular grip. The roasted cobs of corn in the slick coating of butter. The brats. The cream puffs. Who would have thought that this shining vision of wholesome Americana harbored the horror that awaited?

The hour was late when the people began to churn and mill, their voices dropping from the shrill joy of the fair into a maddening whisper of creeping insanity. They slunk past gleaming tractors and out of barns of prize-winning cows. Plates of food were raised into the air, and bodies turned to face the lapping waters of the shoreline, as if the water itself was hungry for the taste of those oozing pastries and hot bites of cheese.

But it was not the water that was hungry.

The first lick of a black tentacle crashed onto the shore, a writhing tendril of madness torn from the depths not of the waters but of some dimension of gibbering madness and unending hunger. It rent the fabric of reality, of sanity, eyes seeing all, tentacles grasping and groping into our world. When they tasted the offerings, the dripping yellow ears with their bursting pustules of sweet corn kernels, the Snickers bars deep fried into crisp and syrupy madness, the cream puffs, the cream puffs, oh the cream puffs it devoured, its body splashed with the white ooze of fresh, fluffy whipped cream. The funnel cakes, like a crispy, powdered sugar-coated creature of the nether dimensions. And the cheese. So much cheese in its crispy shell of fried breading, fresh curds heated and dipped and crunching. The thing ate them all.

It was the food that finally brought Cthulhu from its rest, from its deep and fitful sleep of mad dreams. But then its mind spread out and we felt the knowledge it possessed, abyssal and incomprehensible though much of it was. We knew that it had woken before. We knew the offerings had never been so rich, so perfect. We knew it was here to stay. For it wasn't just this little fair in Wisconsin holding up their offerings. All over the world, foods were raised in the hands of festival goers and Cthulhu was hungry. Cthulhu devoured. Its tentacles reached from those dimensions of unknowable unknowing and spread over the globe, bursting from the sky in exploratory tastings.

And the taste of human flesh could never compare to chocolate-dipped bacon or fried cheese curds.

I have written the details of *that* night, as best I remember them. It is also the great horror afterwards that people often ask me about. What knowledge, as one of the festival goers, did Cthulhu impart to me of its motivations in staying, in laying its tentacles over our planet and ruling over us in its divine, unknowable madness? The things it has done since it arrived, the unspeakable things.

It is true, those of us who attended the festivals that drew Cthulhu from its endless depths felt its horror as its understanding embraced our world. There was, we sensed, endless gibbering madness that clutched and bent the mind as it fell through dimensions. And that was beautiful, in the way that Cthulhu understood beauty. But stupidity and greed, the inability to think beyond the self and the mere moment of current existence. That was abhorrent to Cthulhu. It saw two great powers in the world, now both controlled by something so unthinking, a vacuum that even madness could not fill as it drained and sucked all thoughts into its vortex of stupidity and emptiness. It saw other powers that hungered and hungered and hungered, their hunger even greater than its own, sucking like swollen ticks upon the bounty of the world that Cthulhu desired.

But Cthulhu desired our world, with all its fried cheese and funnel cake and whatever weird delicacies are eaten by the dusky, foreign peoples of this planet. Yet it viewed with disgust all our great leaders, especially those two greatest leaders who so valiantly fought for the purity of their lands. Cthulhu abhorred such concepts and saw the chaos of people moving about freely as a glorious testament to his trans-dimensional madness.

And so the true horror commenced, bringing about the monstrosity you see now in our world. It seems the occasional eating of a world leader is an acceptable sacrifice for some in the name of their "peace." Many of our leaders are dead, not even devoured, simply spit into oblivion. The path to making our country great again has been subsumed in a mass of writhing tentacles, and replaced by the mad visions of a darkly dreaming god-thing. The weak bow before it, praising the health care for all, the mad chaotic vision of a universal basic income, the clutching tentacles of a regulated economy and equality for all people. All in the name of preserving this world, of increasing its bounty that they might make more and more and more festivals with brats and fried cheese and funnel cake. They call it peace. They don't mind the festivals. They don't mind the constant, hot frying scent of cheese-lust. They think the world is better under Cthulhu.

But those of us who have held onto our sanity know that this dark god's mad vision has robbed us of the great leaders who would have divided us into our proper places, given us order, so those of us who deserved the bounties of the world could have them, while the weak took their places beneath us. I write this for you, those last dreamers of sanity. Do not be wooed by these visions of caring for all and economic equality, for controlling global warming and ending wars, all so that Cthulhu might have an everlasting bounty of funnel cake and fried cheese curds with their creamy ichor sauce. Do not descend into Cthulhu's madness. Do not taste of the creamy ichor sauce.

No Collision

by Jennifer Lee Rossman

Jamie sidled up to the bar. It was her first time sidling and she wasn't sure she did it right, but it seemed like an important part of being a cool space captain, the ability to sidle, so she tried her best. Next time, she'd watch some YouTube videos to prepare.

"What'll you have?" the bartender asked, wiping a glass with a rag, because that's the way they did it in the old days and only losers used robots according to the 31st amendment.

She glanced at the menu projected overhead. "What's an orange Russian?"

"White Russian with orange liqueur."

Jamie wrinkled her nose.

"Yeah, it's terrible. Actually pretty damaging to your body, too."

"Then why do you sell it?"

"Someone hacked our ordering system and had it shipped here. A few people decided to be fanatically obsessed with it." He gave a helpless shrug. "You don't drink much, do you?"

"No," she said sheepishly. She'd never had any particular reason to, but to say she was anxious would be like calling the Mona Lisa a nice doodle. Alcohol probably wasn't the answer, but she came from a long line of functional alcoholics who liked beer, and they never seemed stressed, so she figured maybe there was something to it.

"Let me start you off with something easier," the bartender said. "How's an Irish Cofevfe sound?"

"Ridiculous, but I'll try it." Jamie glanced around, wondering if she looked as out of place as she felt. Everyone else seemed so macho, confident. The kind of cisgender white guys they put on the recruitment posters, all perfect hair and the kind of youth pastor smile that tries to convey trust while really silently praying that you don't check their browser history. Real 'Merican heroes.

But she was one of them; she belonged. She had the iron-on patch on her jacket to prove it. And yeah, maybe they'd misspelled "space," and maybe the rocket looked kind of like Mr. Toad, but they didn't let just *anyone* graduate Space Force University.

"You on the ship going out tomorrow?" the bartender asked when he returned with her drink.

She held the glass carefully in two hands and took a sip. Blech. "I'm *captaining* the ship."

He let out a low whistle of admiration. "You don't say. I always wanted to be a captain, but you know how it goes. Bone spurs." The poor man.

A terrible sound streaked through the air, causing

everyone to clamp their hands over their ears and wince. Almost everyone, anyway. One Deaf person in the corner just raised their eyebrows and watched the commotion as the Commander's emergency alert system was used for the fourth time that day.

(The first had been to complain about a very happy young girl trying to warn him about an incoming asteroid, the second was the daily update about which racist nicknames he was using for his enemies, and the third was an accident due to the Commander's enormous hands being unable to press all of the tiny buttons on his phone.)

This time, however, The Commander appeared on screen — on all the screens, from phones to televisions to the menu above the bar — his face contorted like he had just sucked on a lemon. Or, perhaps more accurately, a peach with a mint in it. The man absolutely despised in-peach mints.

"My fellow 'Mericans," he said, sounding extremely presidential. The most presidential. "Some people in the super false, not at all true media claim that one of our spaceships collided with a Russian ship today. This is not the case. No. Did not happen. There was no collision with the Russians."

The screens thankfully cut away from the Commander's face to show a PowerPoint presentation about where the collision did not occur. The pictures were askew and had artifacts that gave it the impression of having been photocopied several times, but Jamie recognized that bit of space near Pluto. That was where her mission was going to send her tomorrow.

There had absolutely been a collision.

It was undeniable, really. Even Jamie, who had never seen a collision between two spaceships, could plainly see that the 'Merican ship had collided with another ship. She did not know enough about flags — at least not the ones that did not represent gay pride — to know whether or not that was a Russian ship, but that was most definitely a backwards R painted on its hull, and she did not think it stood for Toys "R" Us. (Or perhaps that should be Toys "R" USSR?)

"That's a collision, right?" Jamie asked.

Eris, her second in command who also happened to be the Deaf person from the bar, shook their head. "Can't be," they signed. "There was no collision. Just ask…" Here, they made a sign that Jamie did not understand. Her ASL skills were a bit rusty; it looked like Eris was signing "racist sunset rectum" but that couldn't possibly be right so Jamie decided that must be the sign for "most respected Commander."

The final member of their skeleton crew, navigator Diego, leaned against the window of the Starship *Bigly* and laughed. "Funny how they send a queer, a disabled, and a Mexican to do this job."

"Two queers," Eris corrected.

"Right. Either we do it because we can't get jobs back

on Earth, or we don't do it and no one believes us because we are two queers, a disabled, and a Mexican."

"No," Jamie corrected. "The funny thing is that we just happen to have a mission here before the collision didn't even happen, putting us in the perfect position to clean up this wreck we aren't looking at."

"Serendipity," Eris signed sarcastically.

Nothing in the mission statement said that the crew was to clean up the wreck, as that would be documented proof that there was a wreck to clean up. But their ship, supposedly a research vessel despite the administration's utter disdain for science, was equipped with all the necessary equipment for cleaning up a wreck such as the one the crew was not currently looking at, making it clear what they had to do.

With every load of salvage they sent back to the *Bigly* in that solid gold transport pod that they would send to the Amazon for incineration, Jamie hated herself more and more. Almost as much as the Red Hat Society hated her.

(But then, the Red Hat Society hated anyone who dared to suggest that deviations from the ideal allocishet abled white Christian man from an upper-class family could ever represent the real 'Merica. Sometimes she wondered how a club for little old ladies who liked to play bingo while wearing red hats had become a hate group, but she would never know because someone, a long time ago, removed all of the statues and thus erased entire chunks of history from the record.)

"We could take pictures," Jamie said. "We could bring back evidence instead of covering it up. Why are we just ... letting him tell us what to do?"

"Because nobody will believe us," Diego said from the other ship, his voice muffled and echoing in his helmet. "Nobody believed when he appointed his nephew to head the anti-nepotism committee, and we saw it happen on live TV."

Eris appeared in the corner of Jamie's vision, their hand movement as muffled by their gloves as Diego's voice by his helmet. "They would put us in cages, like the babies. No one would listen to us, and we would be imprisoned for the rest of our lives."

"At least the crews of these ships died quick," Diego pointed out. "Sucked through the holes in the ship, exposed to the vacuum of space." And he would know. Diego was from a country that almost exclusively studied holes in ships. A ship hole country, if you will.

Jamie frowned. "I don't see any evidence of these being manned vessels. There aren't even kitchens or crew quarters."

"So what?" Eris asked. "Russia sends up an unmanned vessel, which presumably has a guidance system, and our own unmanned ship just accidentally hit that?" They paused, then added, "Hypothetically, of course. There was no collision."

"Where was the Russian ship coming from?" Jamie

asked, sifting through the rubble by hand, not entirely sure what she was looking for.

"Pluto," Diego said. Pluto. The former 'Merican outpost that was now supposedly overrun with bad hombres? Why would they be in contact with the Russians?

Jamie's hand struck a small object. A flash drive.

"Hey you guys? I think I found something."

"It's a rough translation," Diego warned, "and I have not been able to recover the video file they are talking about yet. But this is something big. Huge. More gigantic then the Commander's hands."

"Nothing is bigger than the Commander's hands," Eris signed. "He says so himself."

"What's it say?" Jamie asked.

Diego hesitated for a moment, reading the transcript again to himself as if to make sure he was understanding his own translation correctly. "It seems... Seems there's a video. They used to keep it in a dossier made of steel for some reason but now they are going to release it. The Plutonians and the Russians. It's a video of the Commander." He paused here. Maybe for dramatic effect, maybe in disbelief. "Now, this is where I wish my Russian were better because I don't know if they're talking about a garbanzo bean or a chickpea, But apparently the Commander spent the night in a Russian hotel room and paid to see one of them placed on a mattress."

Jamie and Eris looked at each other. "Why would he pay to see a garbanzo bean on a mattress?" Jamie asked.

"It might not be a garbanzo bean," Diego pointed out. "It could be a chickpea."

"Well, why would he pay to see a chickpea on a ma —
"

"I don't know," Diego interrupted. "I just know that the people on Pluto think this is important for the 'Merican people to know about."

The three of them sat there, on the bridge of the starship that was so beautiful, perhaps the Commander would be dating it if it were a human, and they debated what to do. Would the public believe them? Would they be imprisoned? Perhaps more importantly, could they live with themselves if they did nothing?

There was only one thing they could do.

Eris hacked the emergency alert system, sending out a message to every screen in the country while Diego worked on recovering the video. Jamie tweaked the alert sound slightly; it no longer sounded like a screeching klaxon.

Now it sounded like someone blowing a whistle.

The Sewer People Stole My Skateboard

by Carlton Herzog

I slipped out around midnight, just as the sun was going down. It was another hot January night in Duluth where the air steamed like a Turkish sauna and the mosquitoes blitzed anything they thought had blood.

Nevertheless, I strutted into that clammy darkness like I owned it. Why shouldn't I? My doped-up parents could care less about what I did or where I went. Tonight, they would role-play in something called the "Good Parents," a holographic tour-de-force right down to the manufactured performances of the virtual kids.

As for the flying squads, they were grounded by the electrostatic charges filling the air from all the dust. But that didn't mean I wouldn't be under my Father's Eye. He could always ping my god-box to get a fix on my location. And a hundred blinking eyeballs belonging to the Citizen's Argus Watch would be surveilling me from behind drapes and blinds. Notes would be taken, reports made, inquiries conducted, and a talking-to would follow. I didn't care. Anything was better than watching those parental fragments of mine pretend to be whole persons.

When I reached the park, I found a rail and did my first grind. A wave of relief washed over me. Skateboarding: I do it by myself, for myself, and I can do it any way I please. Skateboarding is one of the last forms of self-expression left. To know me is to watch me skate. The ride's the thing.

As I did my grinds, I could hear the screams coming from Cement Hill. That's where they send book readers, book runners and book writers. It's an ingenious form of torture: they tie you up, stake you into a form, and then pour cement around you. The torture comes from the daily expansion and contraction of the cement. When it's hot, you bake; when it's cold, you get squeezed. Then there's the crows pecking at your face, the wild dogs chewing on your gut, the parasitic wasps using your belly as a nursery for their young. It's a nasty way to go.

Back in the old days, punishment had an Old Testament vibe to it, draconian but proportional to the crime. If they caught you reading, they gouged out your eyes; if they caught you running books, they chopped off your legs; and if they caught you writing books, they chopped off your hands.

Somebody figured out that while mutilates are powerful symbols of the state's power to punish dissenters, they are also a burden on society. Nowadays resources are scarce, so everyone is expected to pull their own weight. Even the dead get recycled for their teeth (implants), skin (leather), fat (soap), bones (jewelry and lamps), guts (pig feed, dog food), and whole bodies (fertilizer). Some even get live-tossed to the zoo lions. But that's hit or miss, since the zoo lions usually don't last. The ones who do are missing most of their fur and teeth, so while they may let out an occasional roar, the worst they can do is claw and gum you to death as they quietly hope for the extinction of their line.

I can imagine an island filled with all the plants and animals that have gone extinct. I see the mastodons, the rhinos, the tigers, the whales, and the polar bears — just to mention a few — sitting around reminiscing about the good old days before Man made his presence known. I can hear the polar bear chiding the rest: "I told you we should have killed them before they spread. Now look where we are. I'm floating on an iceberg no bigger than a coffee table." Even in the animal kingdom, hindsight is twenty-twenty.

But I digress. After a while, nature called so I put down my board and walked over to the bushes to do my business. As I did, I heard a rustle behind me. I turned and saw a shape hurrying away with my board. I zipped up and followed.

The skateboard didn't mean much to me. My father had gotten it at a garage sale. I could always get another. It was all about the curiosity. Who steals used skateboards?

He was about 70 or so feet ahead of me. In the fading light, I could see that he was dressed in a tattered robe. I figured he had to be a bum. Most bums had been shipped off to the labor camps, but a few stragglers remained. But what would a bum want with a skateboard?

He ran up the centerline of Mott Street. He stopped over a slightly ajar manhole cover. He slid it over, slipped through the opening and then pulled the cover over as he dropped down the hole. I waited a moment to let him get ahead of me, then levered the lid up with my slingshot. I went down the ladder.

The stench was overpowering. I threw up as I stepped into the fetid water. That's when it hit me that I didn't have a flashlight. But it didn't matter because the sewer walls dripped with a luminescent green slime. I waited for a moment to see if my skin would melt, but it didn't. I pressed forward.

I did so despite the stories that I had heard about the peculiar ecology that had evolved in the city's sewer system over the years. Dump enough birth control pills and other hormonal accelerants, dead animals with all their viruses and bacteria, and industrial chemicals, and you create perverse molecular combinations found nowhere else on earth--a Second Genesis of blasphemous life. Nowadays, the urban legends abound with tales of thinking oozes and slimes; swivel-headed horrors, tentacled purple hallucinations; rats with crab claws, fish with hands, and giant slobbering microbes. All you need to do is pop a manhole cover and climb down into that primordial soup to find a shadow biosphere where all manner of creature slips and sloshes along with you.

But whether you believed the yarns about sabre-tooth

rats and two-headed man-eating cats, there was one weird species whose existence couldn't be denied, and it was that of the notorious sewer people. In this chemically obsessed society where there's a pill for every ill, they were the ultimate side-effect produced by Big Pharma's molecular magic.

You see, when the ozone layer disappeared, people began to fry under the constant bombardment of unchecked ultra-violet radiation. Since the air steamed with ungodly heat and humidity, protective clothing was too uncomfortable for outdoor activity. And since the smog scattered and magnified the ultraviolet radiation, even shaded areas offered no protection.

So, Big Pharma concocted Pigmentaphan, a melanin enhancing drug designed to compensate for the effects of undiluted UV exposure. Pigmentaphan produced spectacular results for the majority: it not only allowed them to come and go as they pleased in the not so great outdoors but also homogenized their racially diverse population into a great bronze unity. White people got dark, and dark people got darker.

For a small minority, however, Pigmentaphan had precisely the opposite effect: It turned normal people into albinos. And not just your run of the mill albinos with bleached skin, pink corneas, and vibrating nearsighted eyeballs. By a perverse chemical twist of fate, it snouted their noses, bucked their teeth, and ballooned their foreheads. Over time, every city and town had a cadre of these lurking deformities.

But the worst side-effect of all was that it made them

curious, rebellious and smart. It didn't take long for the authorities to demonize them as the "other." During the day, they hid in the sewers to avoid sunlight and the Blackjacks that hunted them. By night, they would emerge to work their mischief, from tagging walls with revolutionary slogans, to running books.

Rumors abounded. The locals claimed they were baby-snatching cannibals. The Feds branded them enemies of the state bent on overthrowing the government. The religionists painted them as demons operating on behalf of the devil himself. Hollywood made movies about the monsters lurking below our streets.

But for all that, I still didn't care. I could hear skateboard Johnny panting and splashing ahead of me. I followed the sounds. Whenever he stopped, I stopped. I don't know if he knew I was behind him or not. I don't think he cared one way or the other. He was a man on a mission.

Just as I was coming around a bend, I saw him crawl into a service shaft. I had an idea that it led to the old subway line that ran parallel to the sewer main. I was right. But it was not what I expected it to be.

I followed him in, and when I emerged into the old subway station, I was blown away. The subway walls had been painted over. Everywhere you looked, there was an explosion of graffiti. Where there was no graffiti, there was writing in quotation marks. I remember some of them, such as: *"If you want a picture of the future, then imagine a boot stomping on a human face—forever,"* and *"There must be something in books, something we can't imagine, to make a woman stay in a burning house."*

I followed the line down the tunnel. There was enough green slime on the old tracks to keep me from breaking my neck in that swarming darkness. Nameless, abominable things skittered up and down the walls. That was the creepiest part of the whole affair: ominous sounds with no discernible source. It reminded me that the thing I feared the most was the unknown; the things I couldn't directly perceive that were waiting just around the corner to hurt me.

I decided that the best antidote to my fear was to keep moving forward, so it couldn't catch up to me. I moved at a steady pace and took in the macabre sights. Each utility niche I passed was like a little altar. One had rows of ascending benches on which sat human skulls. On the wall, someone had written, *"The words of the prophets are written on the subway walls."*

The utility niches that followed were stockpiled with junk: shovels, rakes, baseball bats, skateboards, crucifixes, frying pans--you name it and it was there. Either somebody was planning the mother of all garage sales, or even a demographic as bizarre as the sewer people had its hoarders.

The skateboard thief had turned down a service tunnel. I followed, and that's when things got sketchy. Rat, cat, and dog skeletons crunched under my feet. Piles of animal remains lined the walls on either side of me. There was the stink of rotting flesh oiled on the aromatic stench of the sewer gas proper. There should be a word for the geometric multiplication of nastiness so vile it makes your eyes and skin burn.

Disturbing as that was, it was nothing compared with what I found around the next bend. Human skeletons, topped with Blackjack caps, hung from the ceiling pipes as far as the eye could see. On one side of the tunnel, I read, *"Remember Caesar, thou art mortal."* On the other, *"Nothing was your own except the few cubic centimeters inside your skull."*

I remembered that some years ago, the Blackjacks had tried to round up the sewer people for resettlement in the Alaskan labor camps. The Blackjacks went in but never came out. They tried it a few more times but got the same result. Some say the sewer people ate them.

I believe at that point, a rational person would have called it quits. To this day I still don't know why I kept going. I suspect that at some level I wanted to befriend the sewer people. After all, the enemy of my enemy is my friend. And I hated the Blackjacks.

One whipped my brother for refusing to salute the new flag on Patriot's Day. A group of those gangsters with badges raped my friend's sister because she supposedly violated the promiscuity laws. So, anyone ballsy enough to kill and eat Blackjacks is OK in my book. Besides, what's a little cannibalism among friends? I kept going.

At some point I began hearing voices ahead of me. They were soft at first but then got louder, then got real loud as if there were an argument taking place.

There was another bend. I could hear them clearly now. They were going on about the skateboard. I crept forward, trying to make out what all the fuss was about.

As I did, I stepped on something that squeaked. I slipped and fell face first onto the glowing slime on the floor.

As I stood up, I came face to face with a sea of extremely pale white faces. Some looked angry. Some were laughing, and others just stared at me like I had three heads. They were dressed like monks and smelled like shit. They had red eyes that fluttered and bounced in their sockets. They all wore coke-bottle thick glasses.

One of them stepped forward and said, "My name is Lockjaw. What's yours?"

I said, "Tyrone Washington".

He looked me up and down and said, "If you've come for the skateboard, you can't have it; it's too important to us."

I was outnumbered so I said "Fine. Keep it. I can get another."

Lockjaw seemed surprised. Then, to the chagrin of his companions, he said, "Do you want to know why it is so important to us?"

Someone answered before I could: "It's too dangerous to tell him anything."

Although I was young, I knew a little about diplomacy. I said, "Look here, Mr. Lockjaw. Your business is none of mine. Unless you intend to eat me, I'll be on my way. You can keep the skateboard. It's no big deal."

Lockjaw studied me, then said to the others: "He's seen us; we have to shut him up one way or the other, and I'm not about to kill him. There's been enough of that already."

A smaller man stepped forward. He introduced

himself to me as Deadbolt. Then he turned to Lockjaw and said, "It's my job to make sure the door between our world and theirs stays *shut*. You did a stupid thing by going up there. And an even stupider one by letting him follow you back down here. That's water under the bridge now. The question is, what's the best way to keep the doorway between worlds shut? If we kill him, they might come looking. They know we're here. They just don't know where exactly. That will be their incentive to pinpoint our location and exterminate us. If we let him into our confidence, then there's a good chance he'll tell them everything we tell him. And they'll come for us."

Lockjaw grabbed my wrist with one hand and put a barcode reader up to my forehead with the other. He read the data: "Tyrone Washington, 224 Fulton Street, father Shamar, mother Tameeka, brother Shamar Jr. If you tell anyone that you saw us, then we'll make you watch as we eat your entire family. Are we clear?"

I nodded.

Lockjaw said, "As for the skateboard, Deadbolt has plenty. I think I saw a new one in the pile behind us. You will take it and go. You will forget about this place."

I said, "We never met."

As I took the proffered skateboard, he said, "Snowflake, see that our guest makes it home; I need to speak with Deadbolt." A long chalk white finger snaked out of a black robe and poked and prodded me forward.

When we reached the manhole, Snowflake stopped me. He climbed the ladder and pushed the cover up and over, then jumped back down. I climbed out and headed straight for the Head-shop. I wanted to forget. So, I fired up my government issue mother of all high-octane cannaboids known on the streets as Chronic, and after a few hits was right as rain.

A Book Club of Sorts

Life continued to happen. I went to trade school every day and half-remembered what they tried to teach me. I was studying to be a Tick-Tock man, a chronometric lapdog who constantly reinvented time standards to keep the people on their heels. That sounds silly until you consider that time is our most frequently used word; everything revolves around time. He who controls the perception and use of time controls the world.

Tick-Tock men are part of the Directed Social Dissonance program designed to weaponize social chaos. Directed Social Dissonance (or DSD) uses social media platforms to keep us fighting amongst ourselves. So long as we are blaming some faceless others, some pernicious thems or bastard theys, we're no threat to the powers that be. Just a band of impotent raging nitwits chasing our own shadows.

Like everyone else, I was apathetic about the whole thing. My eyeballs were permanently glued to the screen of my god-box, where the real learning took place: whom to follow, whom to like, whom to cheer, what to buy, what to eat, what to see, what to believe, what to obey, what to post, what to swipe, and what to tweet.

I was just another rat in a very large Skinner box. But

instead of pulling a lever and being rewarded with sugar cubes, I got the equivalent effect in dopamine each time I played along and confirmed my algorithmically determined identity.

I continued to march in that parade of dead minds, until the day came when I looked in the mirror and saw a growing pig face staring back. It was not a good look for anyone and was made all the worse by the growing chatter in my head. Disembodied voices with a thousand questions I could not begin to answer - the goat with a thousand young.

My immediate concern was disguise. I began to tint my whitening face with dirt, oil and mud. As for my growing snout, I found that lowering my sunglasses on my nose would do in a pinch.

My sanity was another story. They say that in the kingdom of the blind the one-eyed man is king. If by blind they mean dim, and if by one-eyed they mean bright, then based on my experience, that one-eyed man would be exasperated by the knuckle-draggers around him. Man's phones had gotten smarter, even as he had gotten dumber.

I knew that I couldn't stay sane in the upper world, even if I were given some special dispensation to live among the beautiful people. My only recourse then was to retrace my steps back to that underground kingdom of pharmacologically mutated albino monsters and offer to join their ranks.

So, one night, I went back to that manhole cover on Mott Street. I made my way through the maze of tunnels and found the sewer people. Judging from his clipboard and badge, they were eating a certified public informant.

I said, "I need sanctuary."

Lockjaw remembered me. He said, "As I live and breathe, it's little Tyrone Washington. From your looks, I would say you've come to join us."

I asked, "Exactly what am I joining?"

He said, "We preserve the intellectual tradition the way the medieval monks and Arab scholars of old did. But we disguise our books. We impregnate everyday objects with their micro-dot versions, and then we commit the books to memory. In this way, we hide entire libraries in plain sight."

Lockjaw went on to explain that every year the sewer people go on pilgrimage to Tulsa, Oklahoma. Their destination is the Morgan Library. It used to be in New York and once housed the original copies of many great literary works. As the oceans rose, and all the great coastal cities vanished beneath them, the Morgan moved its collection west to Tulsa Oklahoma. Sadly, Fundamentalist mobs burned the New Morgan Library to the ground. The building remains a burned-out shell, but deep within its hidden vaults are pristine copies of the books of Huxley, Orwell, and Bradbury, among others.

"We go every year to pay homage to those prophets and storytellers of old. We travel by night through dark woods and country roads. And every night we gather by a low fire. Sometimes we recite from memory the Classic impressed on the sacred object we carry. Other times, we tell our own stories hewn fresh from our imaginations."

I asked why the government hates books so much.

"You don't give your citizens books for the same reason you don't give your prisoners weights. The fat, doughy, undernourished and listless are easier to manage than the fit. Likewise, ignorant uncritical minds are much easier to manipulate than informed ones."

He continued. "I want you to join us. Over the coming years, your job will be that of memorizing a cluster of original stories. Think of them as the Sewer-bury Tales. You will then teach them to others, so that in the event of your capture or death, they will be preserved as part of our oral tradition, along with their micro-dot counterpart."

The Underground King

One day, as we were cataloguing the goods filched from the surface, Deadbolt shushed me and put his ear to the wall. After a moment, he said, "I count 120 Blackjacks coming from all directions. They must have followed you."

I asked, "So do you have any guns?"

Snowflake laughed, "They'll be too busy worrying about Him to be worrying about us. As for guns, they're about as useful as tits on a bull when it comes to the King."

I asked, "King who?"

Deadbolt said, "The King who rules this underworld. Think of Him as the apex predator. He's what killed all those Blackjacks you saw lining the wall and will kill the ones coming to hurt us. We've only caught glimpses of Him in the dark. He's big enough to fill an entire tunnel. From the front, He's all bulging eyes and slavering mouths with tentacles whipping every which way. Maybe He's something very old that made its way up from the bowels of the earth and settled in the sewer because the hunting was good. Or maybe we made him with our chemical and biological waste. Either way, He's the boss down here, the thing even the darkness fears."

I asked, "How do you know He's a he, and, if so, then why would He protect you?"

Deadbolt said, "We don't know what sex He is. He could be androgynous. And we're not sure if He's the only one of his kind. Probably not, since there's never just one of anything. And He's not our guardian, and we're not His pets. We're just not on the menu. I suspect we don't taste good to him because we are utterly devoid of melanin. It's like the difference between dark and white meat, one's juicy, the other's dry. I know this because I can hear Him whispering in my mind whenever He gets hungry. And when that happens, we snatch somebody from the surface, so He can have a snack."

By now, we could hear the gunfire and the screams. After a few minutes, we could hear footsteps splashing through the sewer water. Then a Blackjack came running toward us, a look of sheer terror on his face. He was no more than six feet from us when tentacle-tipped, star-shaped sucker enveloped his head and dragged him back into the darkness with hardly a peep, just the body parts dragging on the floor. After that, there was only silence.

Deadbolt said, "We'll wait a bit for him to digest that not-so-merry band of would be assassins. Then we'll clean up the mess and hang the skeletons."

As we waited for His Majesty to finish His business, I pondered the finer points of this teachable moment, but the only thing I could come up with was the unsettling proposition that we were saved by nothing more than dumb luck and a nameless evil straight out of hell. But at least we were still alive, and with us, the literary tradition. And that *was* something.

Dark Summit

by Austin Case

The view from the window of Bran Castle is breathtaking. A sliver of moon has crept over the Carpathian Mountains, and its light caresses the tops of the firs, poplars, and oaks growing below. The faintest breeze carries in the scent of early autumn and causes the flames of the candles set on a large mahogany table to twitch. A smartly-dressed man peers out the window towards the silvery horizon. In the moonlight, he notices a single pale dust-mote upon his dark Armani suit and gingerly flicks it off towards the polished, walnut floor.

There is a crash from below, near the castle's entrance. Unfazed, the man glances toward the archway leading downstairs. A massive woman stoops and squeezes through the portal entering the room with a gust smelling of old meat and cabbage. With a fluid motion, she tosses her ushanka hat onto the nearby mantel and slides into a chair at the table in the middle of the room.

"Welcome *gospodină*," says the man.

"Enough with the pleasantries. I'm famished."

The man's lip curls for a split second, but this is immediately followed by a gracious bow.

"Of course." He claps his hands, and from the shadows comes a diaphanous figure carrying a silver platter with a roast pheasant covered in rosemary and apricot brandy. The ephemeral servant places this in front of the woman, then disappears. The woman tears into the pheasant as grease drips down her hairy chin and upon her mink stole.

"You are a gracious *Domn*," she says, mouth full of meat. As the crone continues to gnaw at her dinner, one by one the remaining guests arrive, taking their seats around the table. Some are sleek and young, others ancient and weathered. Some are gaunt while others tower over the feast. More shadow-servants glide to the table with trays of various entrées and libations for the visitors. They then disappear once their tasks have been completed. The motley assemblage dine and trade pleasantries. The host takes his seat at the head of the table.

"I welcome you, my respected guests, to the seven hundred and twenty-first annual meeting of our order. As host this year, I hope you are all thoroughly enjoying your dinner and drinks." The guests half-heartedly murmur gracious replies.

"I know you are all burdened by your respective endeavors, so let us immediately move on to business, so you may all return to your homelands once you have finished with your dinners." This gets a much heartier response from the group.

"That being said, I turn the floor over to the Baba."

The old woman devouring the pheasant takes a deep draught from her goblet of wine, belches loudly, wipes the grease and wine from her chin with the sleeve of her coat, and says, "Right. Business. You are all slovenly cows. Amongst us, I am the only one who is doing any work."

"*Merde!*" says a man in traditional hunter's attire and colors.

"I have been working with the *jinni* in Mosul on a transnational project involving the fundamentalists that he controls."

"I've been doing something akin to that back home," says a stout British man with wild pale hair snaking its way out from beneath a red bowler's hat.

"Not to mention the acts of anti-Semitism I've been orchestrating over the years," continues the man with hunter's clothes.

"Child's play," says the old woman.

"Baba Yaga," chides the host "you must not be so glib. Monsieur Reynard's work is of value to us all."

"Fa!" says the Baba. "I am making ready for wars in my countries while the little dog patters about with vandals." Reynard's lip curls, revealing canines like ice picks, and he gives a blood-eyed stare at the Baba who subsequently spits on the floor.

"Enough!" bellows the host, his powerful baritone shaking the table and its contents. The quarreling guests calm themselves, and with regained composure the host says, "Such pettiness is beneath our kind. We have far more important things to spend our energy on. Now. Though it pains me somewhat to admit, what the Baba says has merit."

Snarls and growls come from the general assembly, excluding Baba Yaga who grins widely and stuffs another large bite of pheasant into her maw.

Brusquely, the host continues, "We have grown slack in our affairs. It has been quite some time since any truly great tragedy has befallen this continent."

"You insult me, *Ţepeş*," says a slender man with a pointed goatee and temple-less glasses. "What you are saying belittles my masterwork."

"Do not misunderstand me Herr Krampus," says the host "what you did with those Jews and gypsies was magnificent. Indeed, a masterwork. But, that was nearly a century ago."

"Have you already forgotten what you and I did together in the Balkans?" asks a slender woman in a grey business dress, wearing sunglasses despite the candlelight.

"Of course not *Kuria* Medusa," says the host "but that was limited to the region and also twenty years ago. Excluding the Baba's domain, what corner of Europe now doesn't enjoy relative peace and prosperity?"

More discord ripples through the crowd. "If I must, I shall point out each of our failings," he continues. "As host I will begin with my own. Sadly, my region has been calm since the end of the Cold War."

"Such failings are your own," says the Krampus, adjusting his pencil-thin tie.

"What can you say of central Europe now?" asks the host. "Your region is one of the most prosperous. And whatever extremists that cause violence in your lands have been pushed to the fringe, largely as a counter-reaction to your 'masterwork.'" To this, the Krampus sneers but says nothing.

"Much the same can be said for the rest of you," says the host. "Monsieur Reynard, though both you and Sir Redcap claim the occasional terrorist acts, they are few and far between. Also, you have outsourced such work to Middle Easterners. Where is your national pride?"

Despite glowers, the host continues, "*Staatsministers* Louhi and Grendel, what have you to offer from the North besides the occasional church burners?" Rumbles come from a pockmarked man-child while a hag in a bone-jeweled leather dress scowls with a frigid gaze that could easily rend a man's flesh.

"What insults shall you hurl at me, son of the dragon?" hisses a withered old man beneath a grey cowl. "My servants still steal fresh children for me to feast upon, not only in my homeland but in many countries across the seas."

"*Caballero* Coco, with all due respect, your ways are old ways. The slaughter of children's bodies and souls by your disciples that kidnap, rape, and murder is a grand pursuit, but its scope is far too narrow."

"Narrow? I demolish families and leave whole communities prey to fears!" screams the old man, causing blood to drip from the castle walls.

"I am not diminishing the value of your work. We

simply must all do more to ravage this continent."

"The work in my home country may well bring economic failure to Europe," says Medusa, her hair twitching beneath its braids.

"That remains to be seen," says the host. "Which leaves us finally with *Sua Santità* Cardinal Monaciello. You, I am afraid are the greatest disappointment of us all."

A tiny and plump old man wearing a red-sashed cassock yells, "I will not endure such disrespect!"

"Our host does make a valid point," says Reynard. His eyes flash with bloodlust at the chance to verbally tear his colleague asunder. "Your work with the church lately has been a complete and utter disaster. Your child molesters are being investigated, and this new pope's progressive platform is atrocious. Not since Vatican II have you reeked of such incompetence."

The cardinal's face turns crimson as he reaches across the table towards Reynard. The host pushes him back into his seat and yells, "I am finished with this nonsense! Reynard, hold your tongue before I feed it to my wolves. Monaciello, if you do not calm yourself, I will squeeze you until your fresh blood pops out of your face for me to drink." The guests calm, and then the host says, "The point that I am trying to make is that most all of us have not been working to our full potential. We have been lax in our endeavors of late. However, I do believe that with a bit more effort from each of us, we can bring about a new Dark Age to this continent."

Skeptical derision roils through the assembly.

"Doubt if you must, but I believe that my suggestions have the potential to rip these lands apart. *Caballero* Coco, your cousin who is in charge of the United States has been doing a spectacularly good job as of late, has he not?"

Begrudgingly the old man grumbles with acquiescence.

"Indeed he has," says the host. "With his influence he has turned a single country that is nearly the size of our entire continent into a powder-keg of potential discord and economic collapse. He has gradually seeded the media and political institutions with fear-mongering demagogues, racists, plutocrats, and war-zealous hawks that have been clouding the minds of their public with an ever-growing sense of xenophobia and naïve complacency." As the host pauses in his speech to take a draught from his chalice, he notes his guests' bated breath.

"I have spoken with him recently about his methods. It was a very enlightening conversation. From our talk, I was able to draw up plans to be used by each of us in our various pursuits." He waves his hand across the table and sheaves of paper appear before the guests. "You will each find a prospectus with specific features pertinent to your respective regions. Each outlines general goals related to ways you can influence your media and politicians, empower hardline conservative extremists, make racist and xenophobic opinions normative, increase the economic gap, and numerous other acts tailored to your regions and more personal interests."

Satisfaction resounds through the assembly as the guests peruse their documents.

"You really may have something here," says Redcap.

"I must admit, this looks very thorough and compelling," concurs the Krampus.

"I think that the entire continent will begin to boil with discontent because of this plan now, not just my own countries," says Baba Yaga. The crowd is pleased enough that only a few guests roll their eyes at the Baba's comment.

"This is a solid plan. I look forward to implementing these ideas," says Reynard.

"I'm thrilled that you are all excited about the prospectus. I think that great things are ahead of us. And on that note, let this meeting be adjourned. As always, keep lines of communication open for any questions, comments, and ideas to be shared between colleagues. We will, undoubtedly, need to work together on certain projects in the near future. I bid you all farewell and a pleasant evening."

The guests shuffle out through the archway, with Medusa lingering.

"You've truly outdone yourself this time, prince."

The host smiles, kisses her cheek. "If I could blush you would surely see my cheeks redden *Kuria*." He bows to her before she departs.

With the room again empty, he walks to the open window and stares out at the moon, which has now risen above the distant mountains. A grin creeps onto his pale face as he swirls the red liquid in his chalice. In the moonlight it looks black. With relish, he savors its metallic taste as it slides down his throat.

"Great things are surely ahead of us."

Their Lips Are Moving

by Allan T. Price

Nicole was halfway through her first patrol of the afternoon, not expecting to see anyone. She'd been a security guard at Matterson Janell Research every Saturday and Sunday for nine weeks, and had only seen the security guards with shifts before and after hers.

A beeping from her phone told her an alarm was triggered. Looking at the alert, Nicole relaxed. It was a room she'd already checked. So, the first false alarm in weeks.

Had she left this door open?

Nicole quietly walked up to the doorway with her taser ready. A familiar looking blonde was standing at a cupboard, examining electronic components. So, not a sensor fault.

Nicole assessed the intruder. Five foot seven, about one hundred and twenty-eight pounds, so her height and five pounds lighter. Not muscular, no backpack and no weapons. The security guard had her taser and a flashlight that would make a good bludgeon.

The intruder was in socks, loose jeans and a t-shirt. What looked like a belt was hanging over her left shoulder, and the zipper on her jeans was broken. Falling down jeans and socks, so no flight risk.

Nicole relaxed a little. "You are trespassing..."

The stranger turned. The thing over her shoulder was a belt, without the buckle, and her jeans were held closed with a cable tie. "Oh. Hi. I expected my shifter to come with me, so I could record my arrival point for five minutes and go back. Haley even installed a button labelled '*Recall*'. But it somehow only transported organic matter. Either Haley or I must have got something wrong at the theory stage. Probably her mistake."

The stranger smiled. "At least I came through intact, not every molecule broken down to separate atoms." She turned back to the cupboard. "As well as the prototype Desaulniers Koch Shifter and my other equipment, I lost my belt buckle, and the button and fly off my jeans. Also my jacket, sneakers and ID." She closed the cupboard, frowning. "And my money and keys, I guess. This room only has about half what I need to build a new trans-shift device. Assuming I can without Haley, it would still take weeks." She walked over to a stool, pulled her jeans up and sat down. "So, I surrender, officer."

"Trans-what?" Nicole wondered if she should tell this polite intruder that she was not a police officer. "Who are you? Show me some... Oh, you claim you left your ID behind. Where? And why do you look familiar?"

The blonde woman sighed. "I left it in my version of Stafford Friedman Scientific, in a slightly different building at three five oh seven, West Fifty -First Street."

"Right address. But this is not Stafford Friedman anything. This is Matterson Janell Research."

"So, Gage Park, Chicago?"

"Yes. And you are?" Nicole tried to commit the intruder's description to memory. Long straight champagne hair, tanned skin and an attractive face. In a 'Mad Max' t-shirt, leaf green jeans with a missing zipper and charcoal socks.

"Dr Desaulniers. Brianne Sidonie Desaulniers. Don't worry, no-one pronounces it right." The woman extended her hand, as if to shake. "Haley and I built this device that..." She gestured at her waist, then smiled, blushing. "That is back in my world, perhaps smoking gently. Probably due to a mistake of mine."

Suddenly, Brianne Desaulniers looked familiar again. Nicole was struck how much she looked like an actress from that record-breaking movie. She couldn't think of the movie star's name, but it wasn't Desaulniers. She looked for a hidden camera. "Is this some TV show prank?"

"No. I'm a visitor from a parallel Earth, who needs help getting home. So, we are in Chicago, Illinois? A Chicago where they speak English, and the North won the Civil War?"

The security guard nodded.

"Where the Russians beat us to the moon, but we got to Mars first?"

"What?" Nicole stared, confused. Then she felt a rush of national pride. "No. We beat them to the moon. In sixty-nine. Kennedy committed us to land a man by the end of the decade, and we did."

"No, he said a moon base by the end of the century and we..." Brianne Desaulniers stopped. "Wow, mankind landed people on the moon in the sixties? Explains why we beat the Russians. Who got to Mars first, and when?"

"No-one has... Oh, you mean probes? We've got two rovers on Mars."

"But no-one even has a Phobos Research Base? Damn. So, who is President? Of the USA, I mean."

"Trump."

"Trump? One of the sons, or nieces, of that billionaire sculptor? Or... not Ivanka, surely?"

"No. Donald Trump, senior."

Brianne chuckled. "No, seriously. Who is President?"

Nicole just stared at her. The blonde slowly frowned, staring back. "Donald Trump? Wow. In my world, the brightest thing about him is his smile. A billionaire now, but kind of a buffoon. Not someone who'd risk his life to help other people."

Sounded like this woman knew Trump. Except for the talk about him risking his life for others. "You claim to be from some alien world? So, you are some kind of..."

"Not another planet, exactly. Another version of Earth. With another version of the USA and Chicago. And another version of Donald and Ivanka Trump."

"And you are another version of some actress or singer?"

Brianne nodded. "Possibly. I released an album in my youth, then had a career on television and in movies. Quit after I didn't get the role in that movie of Twenty-One..." She smiled. "I'm still an actress here?"

Nicole nodded, since Brianne looked familiar. "I think... Yeah. In a Marvel Movie."

Brianne smiled. "I'm still acting because I got a role in the Cinematic Marvel Universe?"

Nicole shrugged, then nodded again.

The blonde sighed happily. "I thought I'd make a good Black Widow. Or Wasp."

"Not sure I believe this talk of alien wo... Sorry, alternate Earths."

Brianne shrugged. "I could show you my driver's license. See if it is different to the ones here. But only organic matter came through. So, unless cotton t-shirts or jeans are different here."

Nicole stared at the woman's t-shirt, which showed Emily Blunt with a shaved head looking grim under the words 'Mad Max - Fury Road'. Hardly proof it was from another dimension, since she'd heard of Emily Blunt and the movie Fury Road. "Come down to the security office. The police can investigate who you are. And whether there are alternate Earths."

In the security office, Nicole gestured Desaulniers to the three visitor chairs and picked up the telephone handset.

Brianne settled down in the middle chair. "So, is Trump clever in this reality? What smart promises did he make to get elected? Has he managed to...? Oh, he must or he'd..." She looked somber and stopped talking.

Nicole couldn't remember where they'd written the

number for regular police calls. "Well, I didn't vote for him." She Googled it.

"But more than half of Americans did? Based on his listed promises?"

"Seven One Three. No. Just under half of the voters went for Trump."

"Are voters distinct from citizens? Are women or the elderly or someone denied the vote here, even if they are legal residents?"

"No. It is just not everyone shows up to vote. Eight eight four."

"Doesn't every American citizen have to...? Oh, lots of people choose '*I don't wish to vote*' in the booths?"

"Three one three one. What?"

Brianne smiled uncertainly. "In my world, not many people do that."

Nicole only half listened to the automated message about staying on the line. "On your Earth, you have compulsory voting? So, everyone votes, and no President Trump?"

Brianne shook her head. "Like I said, no one has to vote." She smiled. "Everyone is simply required to go to a polling booth, or be fined. Been that way my whole life."

Intrigued, Nicole hung up the phone.

Staring into space, Brianne seemed to recite from memory. "In nineteen twenty, less than half of people voted. So, President Harding moved voting to Friday and made it a public holiday." She sounded like she was reciting what she'd learned in school. "So everyone should have been able to vote in 'Twenty-Four. There was still less than fifty-eight percent turnout, so Coolidge tried to make voting compulsory. Lots of other countries have mandatory voting, without it toppling buildings or making people spontaneously combust."

"Voting is enforced if you are registered? Doesn't that discourage....?"

The stranger stopped reciting. "Oh, Harding had already put every citizen on the electoral role. Still, people spoke against being made to vote." Brianne looked Nicole in the eye. "I never understood that. The country is democratic, and these people spend our taxes and decide our laws." She shrugged. "So, the Coolidge Voting Act was watered down. All that is required is to show up to the voting booth. You can put an empty ballot in the box, scribble profanities or write a poem on it. Or select the 'I don't wish to vote' option on the machines."

Nicole realized she still had the police number up on Google. Curious, she Googled voter turnout in Nineteen Twenty and Nineteen Twenty-Four in this world. It was forty-nine point two and forty-eight point nine percent. She Googled the turn out for 'Twenty Sixteen:

46.9 percent of approximately 231,556,622 people did not vote in the 2016 election.

Since she was at the computer, Nicole put those numbers into a spreadsheet. Roughly one hundred and eight million people who could vote didn't bother. Leaving one hundred and twenty-three million who had voted.

She Googled the election results. Trump got forty-six percent of the votes, and Hilary Clinton got forty-eight percent. He was elected by twenty-seven percent of the registered voters. Since twenty-four percent of eligible people weren't even registered in Twenty Twelve, that was only twenty percent of voting age citizens.

So, about a fifth of people voted for Trump, and slightly more for the former Senator and Secretary of State, Hillary Clinton.

Nicole looked at her 'prisoner.' "How do you get everyone to register to vote?"

Brianne seemed confused. "I'm not sure how they did it before Nineteen Thirty-Five. Now everyone has a social security number. I think those records are all you need." She smiled. "If not, the IRS keeps track of everyone, and that way they have to pay taxes."

Nicole returned to what most intrigued her. "What was that about your Trump being the kind to sacrifice his life for others?"

"Our Trump...? In my reality, Donald isn't that kind of person. He is an egotistical sculptor, and still trying to be a movie star." She smiled. "If you film a movie in any Trump building, you have to write a scene for him. Even now he has sold his businesses to his children and taken up sculpture."

"Sold his...?"

Brianne nodded. "Someone showed him he'd have been better off investing in the S&P 500 at six point seven percent and spending his days writing erotica or painting landscapes."

"That can't be riii....?"

The stranger smiled. "In Nineteen Eighty-Four, he

inherited about two hundred million. In Twenty Ten, he boasted of having turned that into eight hundred million. An actress working with him told Donald that if he'd just invested in the S&P 500, at six point seven percent, he'd be a billionaire. Specifically, he'd have one point two billion. So, Donald sold his businesses to his sons for eight hundred million and invested in the S&P 500, and got serious about his acting. When Hefner died, Donald bought the Playboy Mansion and started being a sculptor and free-spirited Bohemian artist. Now he has one point four billion dollars, rather than the two point two if he'd done it in 'Eighty-Four. Still, he boasts of being a billionaire movie star and sculptor." She shook her head, slowly. "But he is not the kind to put his promises in writing or risk his life for others."

"Our Trump, President Trump, is not that kind of person either. He lies more than most politicians."

"More than...?" Brianne stared at Nicole for a moment. "You have lying politicians here? If even a few lie, how is the country not a total disaster?" She unconsciously touched her stomach, as if trying to activate a device that wasn't there.

Nicole stared back. "How is it your politicians *don't* lie? Don't all politicians lie?"

Brienne shook her head. "They've always been honest. Well, all my life. After Nixon was executed for..."

"Killed? No, he resigned, to avoid being impeached."

Brienne, the 'prisoner,' nodded. "In my reality, someone shot him in the street in October of 'Seventy-Three. From memory, Nixon was about to face impeachment."

"Shot while he was President?"

"Executed, for the good of the nation. A team of lawyers, working pro bono, proved it. The basis for this patriot's defense was the defense of others. All the evidence for impeachment was used by the defense team, who argued that any lying politician threatens human lives."

"The assassin was found not guilty? For shooting a president in the street?"

The blonde stranger nodded. "Within a month, new laws were written requiring anyone running for office to submit a list of promises to the Electoral Authority. During the bicentennial, that was amended to require the promises to be 'Smart'." Brianne counted off words on her fingers. "Specific. Measurable. Attainable. Relevant. Timed. So, during the election campaign any candidate for office is required to publicize what they plan to do. It must be specific and timed. Not just job creation or more police, but how many and by what deadline."

Nicole laughed quietly. "This is in writing?" What was the point of politicians writing down their promises, before they broke them?

"Well, most people read the lists on the official 'Electoral Authority Website.' But the law requires one copy on paper, with a bloody thumbprint in the middle. Submitted to the Electoral Authority. Anyone elected who fails to meet their 'SMART promises is executed."

"Executed? Is that a euphemism for...? That their political career is over?"

Brianne shook her head and mimed shooting a rifle.

Nicole went pale. "Wait, you are saying elected officials are actually shot? For the... just for not trying to fulfil all their election promises?"

Brianne shook her head again. "Mostly they are given a humane poison. And not for not trying." She hesitated. "Well, I've never heard of it. Politicians are executed for trying and failing. In the 'Eighties, Wilson promised to balance the budget, and shut down the drug pipeline into Utah by a certain date. She eventually managed the budget by giving up on stopping the drug dealers, and drank the poison."

"Who would run for office, if they can be killed?"

"You mean, executed for failure?" Brianne gave a comforting smile. "Everyone after Lincoln has known they could be killed for being a bold and innovative leader." She shrugged. "Washington, Franklin, Lincoln, Hale and Jefferson would have shouldered the burden, even knowing they could be executed. We should ask no less of leaders now. Politicians are..." The visitor stared at Nicole a moment. "In a rational world, politicians are just like soldiers, firefighters and cops. People willing to..."

"You mean violent? Authoritarian?"

"No. Perhaps the other comparison is better. People who devote sixteen-hour days to a charity. Either way, someone willing to sacrifice their life to help others. Well, the best leaders are like that. Other candidates are simply confident they can do a better job than the incumbent. Some are arrogant and..."

"Arrogant?" That sounded more like a politician.

"Conceited enough they don't believe they could fail. The egotistical or deluded don't see execution as a risk. Others make moderate pledges or even under-promise. Still, if they do what they vowed before the election, no reason to complain." Brianne gave a sad smile. "There was a sharp decline in people wanting to run for office in the first years of the Execution Laws. Then the Bicentennial got people excited about Making America Magnificent."

"So, brave men stand for..."

"Brave men and women. Since the Execution Laws, people running for office have been evenly split between genders and from all races and lifestyles. Being willing to give your life matters more than sleeping with dozens of men or being born of migrants. I just wish Corporate America and Hollywood were as diverse. I might still be acting if Hollywood was less sexist." She sighed. "But in Twenty-Twenty, this America's congress must have... No?"

Nicole shook her head. "It is around eighty twenty, just looking at gender. Sixty or seventy percent white men, and even that is a historic low."

Brianne frowned, shaking her head. "Not many people are executed any more. And the committee gives a pass for not increasing taxes as much as promised."

Chuckling, Nicole corrected her. "You mean decreasing taxes, surely?"

"No." Brianne briefly looked confused. "Lots of people run for office promising to..."

"Promising in writing?"

"Promising in writing to fix the roads, improve the

schools or build new libraries. Obviously, most say they will raise taxes to do it." She shrugged. "Who'd elect someone who claims they will give you both new libraries and lower taxes? They must be delusional." Brienne stared at Nicole's face a moment. "Usually, some candidates promise libraries and higher taxes, others promise not to raise taxes or build new libraries. And people choose between the two options."

"All the people, since everyone has to go to the polling booth, right? Someone can't just stir up right-wingers or the vegans to vote and depend on everyone else being apathetic?"

"People do that here?" Brianne again tried to activate a device she wasn't wearing.

Nicole nodded. "Many candidates will say something that makes six people in ten hate them while appealing to one in ten. That works, if the one in ten work to support them and half the haters get distracted by the next shocking comment by someone else. The extreme comment gains them support and votes. Since one person in four isn't even registered to vote, and forty-seven percent don't bother, the candidate who stirs up a small group will probably win."

"So, politicians can ignore the moderates, the reasonable people? They can just stir up the extremists and the zealots?" The blonde shook her head. "We don't have that. Everyone has to show up, so the reasonable seventy percent of voters will ultimately bury you."

"Especially if you have to make specific promises, in writing." Nicole liked these ideas. "I guess lots of politicians promise not to take money from lobbyists?"

"Lobbyists? Why? There is no problem if people want to persuade politicians with gifts. Long as everyone is open about it. Although it can look bad, taking money to live in big houses, or gifts of sports cars is fine. Some promise, in writing, not to do that. Others see it as corporations, rather than taxpayers, funding a rock star lifestyle. And any politicians accepting gifts and hiding the fact will probably secretly get one from an enemy. Someone who ultimately tells the media. Then..." Brianne mimed shooting a rifle.

"Oh, yeah. Although I was talking about corporations giving tens of millions to spend on attack ads, opinion polls and strategists. Knowing the politician must keep their corporate sponsors happy, and screw over the public. If they don't dance for their true masters, those tens of millions will fund someone who will."

"No. You shouldn't let politicians spend their own... Oh. You don't have public funding of elections? Or a public funded polling company to do Vox Populi? And every..."

"Vex pop what?"

"Vox Populi. Latin for 'voice of the people'. Polls so candidates and politicians know what people want. Corporations too, I guess. Every candidate, and anyone else who is interested, can submit a query and everyone gets the results."

"What about buying ads in important...?"

"Every television and radio station is required to give every candidate, even the lunatic fringe, equal airtime.

Many also give them writers and producers, to avoid showing terrible ads." Brianne stared at the floor, seeming confused. "No-one should be allowed to buy more ad time than someone else."

Nicole decided to focus on one negative of this other world. "You have lunatic candidates? Do they get elected?"

Brianne nodded, frowning. "Buffoons trying to get them elected is becoming a problem. Some irresponsible people want to watch lunatics try to give everyone a pony or make the crippled walk. To try to eliminate all taxes and poverty with credit cards." She shook her head. "Several have been executed, despite clearly being mentally ill."

"So, crazy men are... Sorry, crazy men and women are elected, but not anyone corrupt?"

"No, you don't get elected unless you promise to be open about who finances your fancy car and your junkets. Some of the younger ones wear patches, like Nascar. Corrupt politicians are executed, so not many of those. 'Honest or executed,' is a common phrase."

"How do you spell...?" Nicole Googled her best guess at junket. "Oh. *An extravagant trip or celebration, in particular one enjoyed by government officials at public expense.*" She stood and walked over to Brianne. "I like 'honest or executed.' Our politicians are... There is a common joke in this world. How do you know a politician is lying?" She paused, frowning. "Their lips are moving."

"Surely no one votes for known liars, do they?" Brianne studied Nicole's expression. "Oh. No. They must, or that wouldn't be a common joke. Why do people vote for liars?"

Nicole just stared at her.

For a moment, the visitor seemed lost for words. "The whole basis for democracy, even in a democratic republic, is that you get to choose your leaders. Why would anyone choose a liar? Who is choosing liars so often it becomes accepted that politicians lie?"

The security guard stared, her lips moving noiselessly. She sat down next to her 'prisoner'.

Brianne glared at her. "It's like someone has persuaded you all that every politician lies, so you will just tolerate them doing it. And they are all corrupt, so you don't shoot or poison them for working for the elite or corporate masters." She stood up, hands clenching into fists. "You don't even storm the capital building when ten or fifteen are found to be both corrupt AND liars."

Nicole laughed. "Ten or fifteen?"

"Okay. Five? Three?"

"More like fifty or a hundred."

Brianne sat and sadly hung her head. "And I'm trapped in this hellscape, for weeks." They sat in silence for a while.

"Wait." Brianne raised her head, looking annoyed. "In my world, if ninety percent of people think a breed of dog is vicious, we don't just accept them attacking people. We at least require they be kept behind strong fences, or on leashes. And yet, you don't do that with all these lying politicians ... I mean, why not?"

Dandelion

by K.A. Miltimore

"Nobody loves the head of a dandelion. Maybe because they are so many, strong and soon."
- Tony Morrison, *The Bluest Eye*. Banned in 2022.

Cybill turned up the heat in the coffeeshop. It was a raw November day - the first Tuesday in November to be exact. Not that the date had much meaning anymore. It hadn't since 2024 when Congress had eliminated federal elections for President. Cybill had only been five years old then and she didn't remember the riots, the marches, the tanks - an iron-clad parade down Pennsylvania Avenue. Her mother had told her about it, though, and shown her the few pictures that someone had managed to save before they were purged from the Internet. It became Cybill's bedtime story through the years, more like a myth of a time that was, because officially, the riots and revolts had never happened.

Those days seemed very far away from the rain-washed streets of Seattle. She was twenty years old now.

Her mother died a year ago and none of her friends remembered what it was like before this President.

"How's it going, Cyb?" Darius said, coming in out of the blowing wind, clutching his jacket around him. He was a year or two older and had been the last person her mother had hired before she passed away last fall. She had really liked him.

"Cold, not much business. Hard to attract anyone to the shop with another new RedCap cafe open," she replied, having finished fiddling with the old dial on the wall. They really couldn't afford the heatbill but Cybill was chilled to the bone.

"Yeah, I saw them all in line on my way here today. Plenty of merch in the window for 'good ol' Joes' who like 'American-style coffee'. You see those damn red coffee cups piled up everywhere." Darius stashed his coat on the rack behind the counter. His dark hair was getting long - longer than would be permitted for any employee at the RedCap. Only neat, trimmed hair was permitted there.

"Well, business will pick up, hopefully. There is a shipment tonight and that always brings in a few people." Cybill wiped absently at one of the tables, thinking the mark was a coffee stain. It was a minute before she noticed it was just worn wood.

"Who is bringing the boxes? Helen?" He started pressing espresso for his only cup of the day. Business was bad enough that they could only afford one drink each for themselves.

"I think so. No idea what titles she has but as long as they are before 2020, I want 'em." Cybill gave up on the spot and walked toward Darius, eyeing his drink. She'd already had hers for the day and wished she could make another. Anything to warm up. Hot tea would do. She had some roasted dandelion root that gave a good impression of coffee and it was far cheaper, scavenged from the grass parking strips on Western Avenue.

"I hope they have a lot of textbooks. We've had non-stop requests for those, and we don't have enough to meet demand," he paused to sip the espresso straight from the chipped white demi cup. It was too good to mix with milk; he'd use Cyb's fake dandelion coffee for milk later.

"We'll take what we can get. Any word from Jamal on when the van will be fixed? If it is going to make it to Boise for the drop-ship, he will have to scavenge parts or stick it together somehow." Cybill flipped the switch on the electric kettle and watched the bubbles form at the base of the hotplate. The chopped and roasted root was a remnant from the last summer she had spent with her mother. There were only five or six teaspoons of that summer's stash left and then it would be gone. It had taken both of them to dig out the huge taproot and her mother remarked then that "dandelions send those roots deep; refusing to be moved from their place in the sun".

"No, but he always comes through. He'll patch up the bookmobile and we'll get it loaded and off to the UL before anyone knows the books are here." Darius finished the last of the espresso and let the flavor sit on his tongue. It was borderline unpleasant, so bitter and pungent, and that was why he liked it. None of that lukewarm, mellow crap they served at the RedCap.

The door opened and both of them looked up, stopping their conversation. No one outside of the network should hear what they were saying. Both gave a sigh to see Helen, wrapped up in dark green wool.

"God, what a day. Miserable. I'm parked around back." Helen gave Darius a knowing look. That was his cue to bring in the sealed boxes, out of sight. The sooner the boxes were out of her pickup, the better. She didn't want to be found with them. Delivery day was always the scariest day of the month.

"Hey, Helen. Any trouble?" Cybill turned off the kettle and poured the water over the teaspoon of root in the bottom of a glass beaker. The water transformed slowly into dark roast brown.

"No, I thought maybe I would be pulled over when I got off at Mercer, but the Federal Patrol kept going. Must have been heading to the RedCap for a coffee break." She chuckled and sat down on the stool nearest Cybill. Both women had been students at the homeschool that Cybill's mom had operated in the basement of the shop years ago. The former school was now their Underground Library, one of the biggest around.

"Glad to hear that. I suspect there might have been a problem if they had found you with boxes of pre-President books," Cybill replied, giving her friend a smile. Truthfully, she felt a little queasy at the thought of what would have happened to Helen. Odds are, they would never have known because they wouldn't have seen her again. Time now was measured as either "pre-President" or "post-President". Everything pre-President, 2016 and earlier, was bad. Everything post-President was great. Pre-President books were especially bad. Having them in your possession led to confiscation and fines. Distributing them led to Disappearing.

"Another round of girls were sent to Palm Beach to donate. One of them was selected from Seattle, which surprised me. Don't usually see a west coast girl wanting the honor of providing new blood to the President - or most likely, her parents want the honor. Weird to have a local girl going for the transfusion." Helen reached toward the glass dome that kept the air away from a plate of cookies. She had a sweet tooth for the molasses cookies that Cyb's mother had made for them. Cyb still baked a batch every week.

"Yeah, I heard that on White House TV. I also heard his newest artificial heart was installed and is a tremendous success. Our President will live another hundred years they say, at least."

"That must thrill the VP. He's been waiting for the top job for six years now. Guess he'll need to start his transfusions early if he wants to keep pace with his dad." Helen plucked two cookies from the plate and left a five dollar coin on the counter as payment. The President's smiling face covered almost the whole surface of the gold coin.

"Thanks. Yeah, I try not to worry about what is happening in the capital. I focus on what is happening here, it is all I can manage." Cybill said, taking the gold coin and placing it in the small till box. It was her first sale of the day.

"Hard not to get caught up in all that crap. Tonight is the finale of The Secretary. It's down to two possible Secretaries of War and the phone lines will be open for only three hours. We should know by tonight who the viewers voted for to be the next Cabinet member." Helen, who would never admit this to Cybill, had, in fact, voted by text in the last round of the finals. Her choice had made it to the final elimination and she was eager to watch the results on White House TV tonight.

"Yeah, as Mom would've said, democracy in action - voting by text for the next Cabinet member, using state-owned phone networks. Sounds really transparent to me," Cybill remarked dryly, pouring her steeped root coffee through a cheesecloth filter to remove any debris. She smiled at Helen but the smile stopped at her eyes. Like everything is some reality show, she thought.

Darius came back in, looking like a cat with a mouse in its teeth. Apparently, he liked what he saw in the shipment.

"You will not believe what I found in those boxes. Toni Morrison, Margaret Atwood, Carl Sagan, Douglas Adams, and ten copies of a 2010 Humanities textbook, for starters. Jamal will be thrilled. Boise will be thrilled." Darius sounded like he had just found buried treasure, which he had. Most underground libraries were just that - kept in cellars, basements, hidden rooms. Federal libraries - all above ground and open to registered citizens - carried gleaming shelves of everything published and approved since the country entered the

President Perpetuo era of the Republic. President for Life.

"Nice. He should be here any time." The door opened, cutting off Cybill's words. A young and attractive girl, unknown to the trio, stood in the doorway. She was maybe sixteen. These days, it was hard to judge anyone's ages. Everyone seemed younger in their faces and older in their eyes.

"Hi, welcome to the Taproot. Can I help you?" Cybill said, glancing at Darius and Helen, before focusing on the customer. The girl closed the door behind her and shook off her umbrella. It was a wonder the wind hadn't whipped it inside out.

"Hi. I have walked by this place a dozen times and never stopped in. I thought today would be a good day to get a hot coffee. It is bleak out there." Her voice was just soft enough that Cybill almost couldn't hear her. The girl left her umbrella leaned up behind the door to drip on the mat.

"It sure is. What can we make for you?" Cybill watched the girl give her coat a shake and then shed it like a wet skin, placing it across the back of a chair. She wore a uniform from the local high school; the school was sponsored by a pharmaceutical company.

"Long walk from your high school, isn't it?" Darius remarked, recognizing the trademark crimson and gray crest.

"My dad works near here and I usually come by after class to catch a ride with him. I like to walk. Just not today." She smiled, all teeth, and Cybill wondered briefly when was the last time she had seen anyone smile as broadly as that.

"Oh, nice. Well, what can we make for you?" Darius didn't look nearly as impressed by her broad smile. Darius had a hard time trusting strangers.

"Just black coffee is fine. Nothing fancy," the girl replied, fishing in her pocket and pulling out a five dollar gold coin. She placed it on the counter.

"Just so you know, our coffee is strong in here - we don't go for weak flavor," Darius said darkly. Cybill caught the subtle dig at RedCap in the comment. She'd have to remind him later that customers meant money.

"Works for me," the girl said brightly. Cybill handed her back a one dollar coin, emblazoned with the Palm Beach White House in polished silver.

Darius said nothing as he worked the espresso machine. Helen was quietly eating her cookie, keeping her back to the girl.

"Where do you get your coffee from that makes it so strong?" the girl asked, making small talk as she waited for the hissing of the machine to stop. Darius did not respond so Cybill jumped in.

"Same as everyone else - from the authorized distributors from Puerto Rico. It is in how we roast it and press the grounds that makes it strong. Strength under pressure."

"Neat," the girl said, taking the paper cup that Darius handed her. The cup had a stamp of a long plant root down almost the whole length of it.

"What is that?"

"It is a taproot," Cybill replied. "Same name as the

shop." The girl seemed awfully inquisitive for some high school girl walking to meet up with Daddy.

The girl took a sip, squinting her eyes as she did so. Cybill could tell right away that the girl had never tasted anything like it.

"It is bold, that's for sure. I like it." Evidence to the contrary, the girl smiled broadly again and gave her cup a little lift, like a salute, before sitting down at the closest table. She clearly meant to keep chatting.

"I'm gonna take off now." Helen said, getting up from the stool. Normally, she would have hung out for a bit and said hello to Jamal, but something about this didn't feel right. She wanted to be gone from the coffee shop. She'd done enough for the cause that day. With a slight wave, Helen wrapped herself back up in her green wool and left the shop.

Darius gave Cybill a knowing look. What is he implying, she wondered.

"I noticed some graffiti on your shop front. Normally, graffiti is always something ugly or even dirty words, but yours looks like flowers, in bright yellows and greens. It's pretty. I'm glad the city hasn't painted over it yet." The girl sipped her coffee again, puckering as she tasted the brew, and then smiling again at Cybill.

"You like to talk," Darius said flatly. He was rinsing off the espresso portafilter, getting all the tiny grounds out of the metal. Cybill looked at the clock; in a few minutes, Jamal would be here.

"Just making conversation. I like bright colors and that design on the wall caught my eye. Looks like dandelions. Am I right? I've noticed dandelions on a few places around town. Mostly coffee places. That's weird, huh? Does it mean something special?" She sipped again.

Cybill's mind flashed to her mother, spraying cans of green, yellow and white paint along the stone front of the shop in the dark of the night. She'd created an angular pattern of growing dandelions, in full yellow roar, with a floating halo of the white fluff - the capitulum - scattering seeds in the invisible wind. For some reason, no one had ever come to paint over it. Over time, a few places around town had little flashes of dandelions on their storefronts too. Places in the network or places where you could avoid the prying eyes of the KAGs.

"Gardeners want to rip them out, get rid of the common dandelion, but it survives. The taproot is deep and if you try to rip away the heads, it only scatters the seeds further. Dandelions last." Cybill's mother had told her, in between coughs. In a few more months, the cancer would take her, but her graffiti was still there.

"Yeah, they are dandelions. They make good tea," Cybill said, blinking herself back into the present, with the blonde girl looking at her expectantly. Darius had slipped out from behind the counter and was locking the door.

"Look, kid. You ask a lot of questions. Maybe you better just take your coffee to go. Not to be rude or anything but I don't like folks who come in all chatty-like." Darius sounded angry and Cybill gave him a stern look. What the hell was he doing to a paying customer?

"Darius..." she started to say but the girl interrupted

her.

"Yeah, sorry, I hear that a lot. Guess I am nosy. Didn't mean to annoy you. I was just curious." The girl stood up and gathered her coat, keeping the coffee cup close to her as she grabbed her small book bag. Darius still stood between her and the door.

"Not to be impolite, but do you mind letting me take a look in your bag? It's not that we don't trust you but we don't know you and you come in here, making us all nervous and well..." he chuckled, but there wasn't any warmth to it. He reached out and took her bag before she could respond.

"Whoa, Darius. That's enough. What the hell are you doing?" Cybill came out from the counter and stood next to the girl, who started to protest.

"Gotta make sure, Cyb. Gotta be sure." Darius said, opening the canvas flap and sliding the contents out on the table. Two high school textbooks landed with a thud, each emblazoned with the school's logo and the President's face. A small red notebook slipped out from the inner pocket. He flipped it open.

"I knew it. She's KAG. It's their notebook. She has the shop name down with a bunch of others." Darius tossed the notebook down and crossed his arms across his chest.

"I can explain, okay. Look, that notebook is my dad's but I was jotting down places where I saw the dandelion art. I want to go to them all and find out what the dandelion means, that's all. The notebook was just some spare paper at the house. Honestly, it's just paper." The girl's voice sounded panicky but sincere. Cybill would have guessed she was telling the truth, but these days, who knew what was true anymore.

"Sure," Darius said, stepping toward the girl. "A teenage girl just happens to have a watch list in her school bag and it is all innocent, right? That sounds totally reasonable." Cybill didn't like the look on his face.

"Darius, enough. Let her get her things and go. We aren't the thought police. She hasn't hurt us," Cybill said, feeling the girl lean back toward her. Darius was closing the space.

"No, Cyb, that isn't enough. We can't risk it. You know why. Not for one of them." Darius said, and Cybil knew he was serious. He was going to do something to the girl. He was worried she would jeopardize the network. Cybill reached out to pull the girl behind her but she was quicker, pulling out a can of mace from her coat pocket.

"Yeah, no. I don't think so. You are going to let me go, now. Or I am going to use this. Don't make me use it. I don't want to but I will." The girl held the can toward Darius with her fully extended arm, inches away from his face. A blast of that would incapacitate him for hours, no question. Maybe worse.

"Hey, everybody, calm down. This is crazy. We aren't going to escalate this, okay? Darius, back up. Girl, whoever you are, no one is going to hurt you. We're talking, that's all. Everybody calm the hell down." Cybill's voice was too loud for standing that close. If Jamal got here and saw this scene, things would likely go from bad to even worse.

"Talking doesn't work with these people, Cyb. You know that. They don't listen. They don't hear anything but what they want to hear. One big frickin' echo chamber, that's it." Darius said, though he did step back, giving the girl a few more inches of space. Her arm never wavered.

"So your answer is this, Darius? No. Don't assume the worst, okay? People can be curious. People can make lists. People can wonder about dandelions. None of that is wrong. Can we remember who we are for two minutes? When did curiosity and questioning become a bad thing with you?" Cybil's hands were easing toward the girl's arm, though the girl couldn't see it. If she was lucky, she'd be able to get the mace away before she could push the button. She only had minutes before Jamal would arrive.

"It became bad when her questions could land me in a black site somewhere. I don't need snoopy kids causing me to Disappear." Darius said, pressing slightly forward again. Cybill could tell he was about to make a move as well. She thought she heard a car door slam out front.

Cybill grabbed the girl's elbow in one hand and her can of mace in the other, ripping her finger from the trigger before the girl could press it. She heard the girl scream as the mace left her palm. Cybill had it, leaving the girl caught between a spray of mace and Darius. He started to move from the door.

"No, stay there, Darius. The girl is going to get her things and leave by the back door and you are going to stay right there. I'm not doing this. I gotta believe that we can just be normal people, who disagree on things, who believe in different ideologies, and who let other people live their truth. I'm not letting anything happen to her. Mom wouldn't have let this happen. Kid, get your stuff." Cybill said, giving the girl an abrupt nudge with her empty hand. The girl quickly pulled her items from the table and stuffed them in the bag.

"I hope you can understand that the world sometimes gets the better of us and some people let fear confuse them. I hope you remember that and I'm sorry things got out of hand back there." Cybill heard Jamal knocking on the front door. If he came inside before the girl left, he probably wouldn't let her leave.

"Thank you for letting me go," the girl said, following Cybill, who quickly led her to the back door. Darius must have unlocked the door and let Jamal inside; Cybill heard angry voices behind her.

"You better run now. Go home." Cybill said, watching the girl sprint off into the wet wind, down the darkening alley. If she kept running, Darius and Jamal wouldn't catch her.

"What the hell, Cybill?" She heard Jamal's voice calling behind her but she didn't turn to look. She wanted to make sure the girl had a head start. Two blocks down, the girl's figure turned the corner out of Cybill's sight. The girl wouldn't tell anyone what happened, would she? But just in case, they better get those books out of here tonight.

Around the block, the girl stopped, catching her breath and holding her bag to her. A dark gray sedan, idling at the curb, pulled closer to her. The driver pushed open the passenger door from inside. She slipped into the warm interior and the car pulled away into the evening traffic. The small new American flag bumper sticker glowed red from the taillights.

The Children Who Lived on the Stairs

by Jill Hohnstein

I stopped. The firehoppers[1] stopped, and then they turned their creepy little heads to look up at me before going dark.

Ha ha, Goobs, nice one. I waved in the direction of the plastic[2] bugs before checking behind me to make sure their path was disappearing. Nothing but darkness. Good.

I closed my eyes and listened. I could hear low voices

---

[1] From what we can tell, this planet did have something like fireflies in its western hemisphere. We believe these bioengineered insects were modeled after a sort of hybrid firefly-grasshopper. Unclear if based on a biological insect.

[2] This substance doesn't quite have the same atomic structure as plastic, as you know, but "plastic" is the closest word we have.

about 100 metres[3] ahead.

Deep breath in. Silent Oowh[4] out. One foot and then the other. Following the glowing droppings left by the hoppers.

Purple,[5] because Goobs knows it's my fave.

Goobs is the actual best, but oh, man, when he first came to The Steps and wanted to be called "Indiana?" Such a nerd. Thick glasses that made his eyes too big and like he was super happy all the time. Rolled up pants, for God's sake. No, you're a goober. Yeah. I know. Not very clever, but it fits him.

Anyway, turns out, he's the smartest one of us. And most of us are pretty smart. He's all about the biotech, which helps us a lot. Like,[6] the king[7] closed the research labs, right? 'Cause he's too dumb for science. I mean, like,

---

[3] Their unit of distance is astonishingly close to our metre, so for ease of interpretation, we are using "metre" in this text instead of the translated "nosnos."

[4] We found a reference to this term in religious texts, and it appears to be used in meditation. Given that it is a descriptive sound, we think, we are using the phonetic translation here.

[5] Probably purple, but it could also be blue. This word is frequently used to describe the sky, which we perceive as purple, but, as we have seen, the sky changes color.

[6] The original word is a verbal tick, we believe, similar to "like" as used on Earth.

[7] Actually more of a governor, but her word indicated royalty. We're not sure why.

there were no guards because the dumbshit[8] took the money that was supposed to go to pay the guards. And, OK, sure, Goobs can pass AND he looks like he's about 9,[9] so he gets away with everything. I mean, seriously, he told the one guy — we don't know who he was but Goobs said he had clean clothes, so probably an actual criminal — that he just wanted to grow corn for his sister and the guy was like, "Sure, kid." So Goobs walked out with seeds and chemicals and animal parts and I don't even know what else, and now I have personal glowy, jumpy pathfindy bugs.

I was wearing moccasins and my steps were silent. I could still hear them, though. That's how good my hearing booster was. Yeah. And good enough to hear an animal about 50 metres to my right. Slow, cloppy. Probably a deer.[10]

Good.

I shouldn't have to kill it.

Deep breath in. Silent Oowh out. Deep breath in.

---

[8] Approximate translation.

[9] Approximating ages is difficult. Ages aren't frequently referred to in the religious texts, official documents and so forth. And we think their years are much shorter, but the conversion isn't consistent. We believe relativity is taken into account. The original number here was 74, which we're guessing corresponds to our age 9 years.

[10] When referring to animals, we chose the closest Earth relative. This "deer" would probably have had a much longer snout.

Silent Oowh out.

The deer, a doe, walked into view. She looked at me. I'm trying, little girl, I thought. We're trying, OK? But you have to leave now 'cause I don't want someone to hear you and find me, so I will have to kill you and I'm really, really not a killer.

Well, I mean, I am, but just of people.

Stomp stomp. Schhhhc bam. Groan.

What the f—?

"Excuse me. Sorry. I was told to —"

"—I. Don't. Care. I'm sleeping and you need to go away."

I shifted my head enough to look up with one eye.

"Well, that's what I'm trying to do, but I have to go up and this suitcase is heavy."

Suitcase? I opened my other eye and looked up at a girl about my age, 9, maybe 10, with skin even darker than mine and greenish-yellow eyes and a giant red[11] velvet[12] suitcase. I couldn't help it. I laughed, which woke up Trihn-isi and John-da.[13]

---

[11] Again, color is an approximation.

[12] Unclear if they have manmade fabrics.

[13] Naming conventions take into account skin color and gender, that much we have discerned. However, it's not clear how many genders there are. So far, we have counted 12. Conrad Williams is researching gender in-depth and should have a report at the end of this month. For the remainder of this

"Ree? C'mon," Trihn-isi shout-whispered from the landing below mine.

"You guys, this *zunkai*[14] has a freakin' suitcase."

The girl sighed and smirked at me. "Yeah, make fun, *fspach*[15]. But I got clothes for everybody and shoes and a wireless router for somebody named Benka-osi, and stuff for potions and maybe something for you. Just get me to 14 and we'll figure it out tomorrow."

I shot out of my sleeping bag and grabbed her by the neck. "Never call me a *fspach* again or I will kick you until you're dead." I held her stare with my own. "Understand?"

She looked like she was about to cry, so I let her go. Cough. "I won't." Cough. "I promise."

"OK," I said with a shrug. "Good enough." Then I helped her drag her suitcase four more flights up.

And that was how I met The Witch.[16]

She's my closest friend now. And she loves to make little bottles of essential oils from the plants she finds. We have medicine and perfume and salves to help heal cuts. Oh, and poison.

---

text, we randomly assigned pronouns based on our current gender binary. Oranges have names that end in -a or -si. Pinks' names end in -o. For the remainder of this text, we will remove the suffixes.

[14] No translation. Probably offensive.

[15] No translation. Probably offensive.

[16] The narrator calls her dearest friends or closest companions by their nickname, but others by their (we think) given names.

I like the woods. I like how quiet they are, but so full of life if you know how to see and hear it. The City is so noisy, and I bet it will get worse after. Up north, we have a place in a meadow, but it's near the woods. I think I'll put a tent there. Me and Mama, if I find her.

I'm Vijria. My friends call me Ree and The Witch calls me Reader. It's cute; I like it. I'm 11. And, yeah, I kill people sometimes. I mean, like, not as a hobby, but as a job. Some people have to be killed. That's how it is. A lot of people are bad. Not animals, though. They're mostly good. The deer, by the way, is still alive.

I wonder what you're thinking right now. That I'm psychotic? That I'm sad. Do you feel sorry for me?

Remember that time that my parents were taken from me and put in camps and nobody did anything about it and my mama is probably dead and my papa almost certainly is? Well, we're doing something about it since you all couldn't be bothered.

Man, you should have heard yourselves. "We need to be civil about this." And for real, "Violence will only make us like them." I mean. I don't know, maybe you watched too much entert[17] or something, but that's not how real life works.

And then:

"We'll VOTE. Let's VOTE."

---

[17] Similar to a 3D, we believe this is a holographic television show that would also have some live action depending on where it aired.

Yeah, thanks. That worked out swimmingly. 50% of the rainforest is gone, so, I mean. You guys screwed up and are still screwing up.

Now me and my friends are trying to save our families, if they're even still alive, and the rest of this garbage country, and the world, maybe, so we don't have to watch you all kill the good things, like water and penguins and real-life fireflies and us, OK?

And someday, I'd like to go to a parade again. Catch some candy, get my face painted, laugh at a clown.

I'm a kid. I'm still a kid. We're all kids. 9 and 12 and 11 and some as young as 6.

We're figuring it out, though. And planning? You guys and your enterts made it all seem so hard. We're doing this in—never mind. I can't say anything else.

So, In about 45 minutes[18] I'll know if the pressure bombs work. Pretty much all of tonight is hinging on that. Bomb bombs would be too loud and flash bombs would be too flashy. Pressure bombs, John came up with these, obviously. Quiet and invisible.

Breathe in. Breathe out. I have anxiety now. Because of hormones — I read about my cycle — or maybe 'cause of the end of the world. One of those. John is our bomb girl, which means we have all put our trust in him,

---

[18] We still don't quite understand how their chronology work. It wasn't quite linear or evenly measured, so for simplicity's sake we're going to use minutes in this text.

mostly. There are plans if the bombs don't work – not great ones, but still, they exist. My plan, if the bombs are miserable failures, is to run the hell away.

I'm not going to tell you where I am. But tomorrow, if this works, you'll probably figure it out.

The firehoppers were programmed to find the easiest path to the cabin and to keep me away from any of the guards until it was time to take them out. They stop, I stop. And they were stopped. They went dark again and I could hear them hopping away in all directions. Then just like that, they returned and led me to the left, leaving tiny glowing dollops behind in case I lagged before they noticed. Seriously, Goobs is a genius, because the marks disappeared after exactly a minute. No clue how he did it.

The hoppers stopped again, this time to remind me to check my pack.

Earguards. Water. Cornapples. Phone in case my watch breaks. Food. Spray (something deadly The Witch insisted I took). Face mask. Bomb. Bomb. Bomb.

John. John came to The Stairs about 6 months after I did, the day after Mirrcew.[19]

Benk, Goobs, Trihn and I had talked about maybe making a ruckus and getting people out of the cages. The

---

[19] A harvest holiday

twins, Joel and Olivia, who liked to visit the other Stairsers, said they were talking about it, too.

"Well," I said, "I guess we should talk together. Liv, do you wanna?"

"Yup," Livia nodded. "I'll go talk to them tomorrow."

And then John showed up in a freaking princess dress, carrying a duffel bag and a yoga mat. She was wearing make-up and, I am not even kidding, high heels. Their hair was in a bun and he was chewing on a stick.

"Hi. I'm John. She/her, he/him, they/them." John held their hand and Benk and I helped him up.

"All of them?" I asked.

"Yes," she said, "And change it up. Like, don't always call me she, k?"

"OK. Where are you from?" I asked.

"Here." He gestured around.

"Where were you before?"

"Subway."

"Oh gross." I don't like being underground and I don't like rats.

"There are a lot of us down there. It's safe. But we heard about kids living outside buildings. A few of us decided that outside was better. Yours was the first I saw, so here I am."

"OK," I said, "you can have 18. We eat on the roof. Clem, the owner, brings us meals."

"So if you don't have to look for food, what do you DO all day?

"We play games, read, and try to figure out how to save the world."

"That's cool. I happen to have some ideas," they said, and lifted up his skirts to show me the four guns strapped to her legs.

"Oh."

"Yeah."

And that's the story of how we got a weapons expert.

We were illegal then, of course. Well, I mean, we still are but we're mostly invisible now.

Illegal in that we had curfews. We had to be off the streets by 8, but most of us didn't have homes, so we'd either end up in jail or shelters, which were worse than jail, if we got caught. Those of us who are still out learned to hide. In abandoned buildings, with sympathetic Pink families, in the subway, in the woods. Some of us ran away to ... I don't really know.

Anyway, I got caught stealing food from a Starbucks, but before they could call the cops this woman said, "Oh, THANK you for picking that up for me. I realized that I forgot to send money." And she paid for the cake pops and the fruit rolls and the cold brew I was trying to walk out with. I froze and stared. She was like 6 feet tall, bright pink and had long silver hair and sky-blue eyes. She looked at me and smiled. "Come with me," she beckoned. "I figured something out."

The Stairs. She figured out The Stairs.

Pinks are barred from harboring us, although some did anyway. They would end up in the camps if they were caught doing so. Which, turns out, was an effective deterrent.

But Clem found a legal loophole. She let us make our home on the old fire escape outside of her building. The royal guard couldn't trespass on her property or they could be shot. I guess weapon "reform" was good for something. And we were clearly not hidden.

I accepted her offer and was soon joined by Trihn, Benk, the twins and everyone else.

Orange children, living on the outside of buildings on decommissioned (I just learned that word) fire escapes and traveling by rooftop. As long as we were on The Stairs by 8, we were safe. I mean, you know, as safe as we could be. It gets cold in the winter. We manage, but sometimes one of us doesn't manage well enough.

Anyway, that's why 18 was open and John was able to move in.

I was about 40 metres away and could see the lights of the cabin now, so my task was to wait until I got the all-clear from the other teams, in about 30 minutes or so. Goobs's firehoppers went dark, but would reactivate when it was time for me to find my way out. Or I would find a flashlight, or be dead.

Goobs, like I said, was probably a true genius. He knew about shit that I will never understand. He made the bugs, obvs, but also this crazy quick-growing corn-appley hybrid that he planted in garbage barrels full of soil on the roof. And he figured out how to grow landfish, which I will not eat, and even made us a kind of dogcat that lived on the roof. Harv-osi.

We didn't really need the food right now, but he kept seeds for after.

Goobs would go to the lab he built during the day and come stay with us at night, even though he didn't have to. But it's good he did.

Don't get me wrong, Trihn was smart, too. She got us connected to the internet and figured out how to use existing transfer lines. Then she and the guy from the West built our own system by hacking a satellite. I have no idea how, but I have a phone and a watch that's basically like a phone, but smaller.

I'm not that smart. I can read palms and the Buoldo,[20] because it's fun. And I'm really good at hitting things I aim at. Like with an arrow or a bullet or a piece of gum. So I'm out here getting ready to kill one of the primary targets. Not the king, though. The Witch wanted him. Poison, of course. In the water lines. In the water and then evaporating into the air. How freakin' easy was that? Gonna kill the whole house, and probably some of the neighbors. I suppose they're dying right now, actually. Cool.

In our old lives, we had school and family and friends that took up our time, and in our pre-Stairs lives, we had survival. But life on The Stairs was, I don't want to say boring, but it was boring. At first, we went on stealing sprees, but didn't have any place to hide the loot. And we

---

[20] Something like our Tarot cards.

were less risky. We weren't hungry. We didn't have our computers and entert was mostly commercials and news.

So we learned.

It was Benk's idea to break into the libraries and schools, although, to be honest, it wasn't that hard. We stole books and magazines that no longer existed and games and tools. Trihn learned about hacking. John learned about weapons, Benk read about strategy, The Witch learned what herbs healed and what herbs hurt, and I wasn't interested in anything, so I learned stuff that went well with what The Witch was doing.

And I'd practice hitting things with other things.

We all learned meditation.

2 years.

Once Clem opened her stairs to us, the idea spread. Stairs, porches, back stoops. Anything connected to a building became safe spots for us. Pink people in other towns and cities followed suit and soon it was A Thing.

In the cities, the rooftops were our sidewalks.

We met and planned and Goobs accidentally became a sort of leader here, Hwij-isi was the head of the West cities and the twins ended up South. There are others scattered around who are involved, but the big shit is going down... well, you'll know soon.

It seems fast now, but two years is a long time when you're living outside.

Before we had phones, we had to talk in person. The runners, the kids who rode their bikes between towns or found rides with trusted adults, had the scariest jobs, I think. But we only lost two. Probably to the camps, maybe dead.

We didn't fight over who would be in charge. You think we would, because you all do, but most of us didn't want to. Maybe Hwij did. Goobs didn't, but he's older and just kinda fell into it. Plus, he looks Pink and is articulate, even though he's small. People, adults, take him seriously.

He and Clem are the ones who decided we needed mayors on our side. Mayors. Brilliant.

The big cities are going to see the most chaos and there probably won't be a lot of communication. I mean, we'll be fine. We have a compound, I guess you call it, waiting for us in the North. And we'll have food and lots of weapons.

But the communities here will be looking to their mayors for help and comfort. So they're our people. Not hard to do, not with Trihn and Uan making sure the elections went the way they were supposed to. And Clem had friends, who developed a sudden interest in local politics.

Adults, of course. Nobody was going to elect a 11-year-old, get real. But everybody wants a Pink woman in charge these days, so we took advantage of that.

The races were close and we had to let some of our candidates lose in the smaller cities, but we have mayors and a few governors, and they're going to take over while we, and anyone in our families that we can find, head up to our new home. You're going to have to figure it out from there.

You. Yes, you, reading this. We don't want you with us, by the way. And we'll keep you out.

OK. First big check-in. They worked. John's pressure bombs worked and eight of the dukes and duchesses have been put down. The Witch sent one of Goobs's spybees into the house to look for life. It's a big house, so we won't know everything for a while, but it looks like her poison did it's magic, so to speak.

My turn.

I can do this.

I quietly took off my pack and watched the firehoppers flicker out. I was close enough to the cabin that I no longer needed them.

I pulled out one of the pressure bombs and set the timer. I put the earguards around my neck and walked until I was about 20 yards out.

I stayed silent and gently placed the other bombs in their positions.

All I had to do was push the detonator and wait 5 seconds.

Deep breath in, silent Oowh out. Ear boosters off. Earguards on.

Button pushed.

5 - 4 - 3 - 2 - 1

I felt it. A little bit of vertigo. Then nothing.

I moved closer and I could see the guards outside falling. Some would come to and the other bomb would put them out again. Some ... would not. Part of me was glad my target didn't want to pay for better security, but part of me felt bad for the men and women here tonight. They might have been better people in different times.

I grabbed guns from the two closest to the entrance. Nobody inside noticed a thing. The TV was on, and I assumed it was loud.

The next part was easier than you might think.

The four of them were watching some reality TV show. They didn't look evil. They looked normal.

It only took two seconds. I didn't see their faces.

I shot the minister[21] first. I shot his mother. I shot the princes[22] before they could turn around to see what had happened. 4 shots. I'm really good.

Then?

I dropped the guns and walked out the door, with Goobs's firehoppers leading me back to my bike.

Now we're on the way to meet the prisoners and look for my mama.

---

[21] Possible mistranslation, but we think it was somebody important in the government.

[22] Possible mistranslation, but the word used here had the same root as the one used for "king" earlier, even though this civilization doesn't appear to have ever been a monarchy.

I don't know if I'll tell her what I did right away. Maybe someday. I'm scared she won't be proud of me.

I hope she's alive.

Anyway, I'm writing this down and I'm going to leave it for you to find. I'm not sure what's going to happen tomorrow. But, everything will be different, for sure.

We killed all of them.

We did a lot of bad things that might be good things, I think. I hope. Man, if this is what being an adult is like all the time, it's no wonder you guys messed it up so bad.

Anyway, good luck.

And, you're welcome.[23]

---

[23] This is where the account ends.

Ballad of the Swamp Refugee

by Kurt Newton

They came trickling in like a new kind of
migrating bird, even before the Wall went up,
young and old and little ones hiding deep in
the swamp.

You know people are desperate when they'd
rather take their chances with the gators and
the snakes than with the white folks and their
badges.

But then Julius and I were understanding of
not being accepted by society. So we took in
as many as we could and taught them how
not to get eaten.

In the old times, nobody needed no papers to
prove if they belonged. They is here right? And
nobody goes to a place where they don't want to
be, that should be proving enough.

But, no, somebody got it in their head to make
everyone pass a test. You pass the test, you in.
You don't, you out. And it's been that way
ever since.

But here in the swamp there's a different kind
of test. It's the same for everyone. The swamp
lets you know if you in or you out. And these
new birds settled in just fine.

They planted rice in the shallows, beans and
tomatoes between the trunks of cypress trees.
They hunted gator and made a swamp tequila
that stole the breath from your lungs.

It was a nice time for Julius and I out here in
the swamp to see these people so full of life
and love grow up around us like a garden made
of hope. A nice time.

But soon Julius and I will be gone and these new
birds will be left to bury our bones. Until then
we'll just have to keep an eye out for the snakes
and gators and make the best of it, together.

Shrinking

by Taliyah St. James

"We're short again," John said.

Aimee whirled from the sink to face him, her hands already beginning to tremble. "How?"

"Water bill was high and taxes went up again." As he spoke, John took a step back and gave a little shrug. Aimee didn't miss his frown at the still-running faucet. She didn't miss that he had barely looked at her, let alone touched her, in days, either. She slapped the handle down and paced the kitchen.

"How did this happen? I have a good job. You have a good job. How did we go from beautiful apartments in high-rise buildings to this?" She gestured to the 1990-something Pre-Modern home they were renting.

When they had first started dating, Aimee had lived in a newer condo, one that regulated everything so the utilities never got out of hand. One that had a transport tube in the building, an auto-cooker, an immersion system, and every other luxury. She had agreed to move with John into a house in the Pre-Modern district so they could save money to buy a home. It had been a year since they'd hauled their belongings into the dingy ranch, and they hadn't managed to save a penny. Somehow, even with her salary as a geneticist and his as a private accountant, they barely scraped by.

His look softened and with slow steps he walked over and wrapped his arms around her. "Sorry," she whispered into his ear. "I know it's not your fault." She couldn't say it out loud, but she knew it was hers, hers because she washed the dishes every day instead of wiping them off like their neighbors did, hers because she read by lamplight instead of going to sleep at sundown.

She led him into the living room and flopped onto the couch, springs groaning under their weight. They sat on opposite ends, staring at each other. She reached her hand out and laced her fingers through his. "What do we do?"

John pulled his hands away and covered his face. His sandy hair bouncing as his shoulders trembled. When he looked up, his eyes were clear, his soft jaw set in a hard line. "Babe, you need to Shrink."

Aimee shot to her feet. She pulled her hair from its ponytail and ran her fingers through the auburn curls. "You're joking."

"I..." He paused, his mouth a thin line. "I've already gone twice. I can't go again."

Aimee crumbled onto the couch. "Twice?" She swallowed hard and dug her nails into the faded green couch cushions. "Why didn't you tell me?"

"I thought everything would level out. I didn't want..."

John trailed off and gave a small smile. "I love you..."

She closed the gap between them and burrowed her head into John's chest. This explained his distant behavior. He had tried, no matter unsuccessfully, to shoulder the burden alone.

"How much?" she asked as she sat up. She focused on the blue of his eyes, knowing the light in them had dimmed only temporarily.

"Only a quarter," he said as he squeezed her shoulder.

A quarter. A quarter was nothing. She could grow that back in no time.

"Okay," she said. "I love you enough to love you less."

"I love you enough to love you less," Aimee whispered as she walked along the sidewalk. She had never liked the phrase. For most of her life, she'd only heard the words uttered in romances. An over-the-top statement spoken out of desperation.

After moving into the Pre-Modern neighborhood though, she'd heard the phrase again and again. Between couples and throuples, from parent to child. Unlike the fantasy versions of the line, the people here said it less with desperation and more with an iron determination, as though the risk Shrinking carried was too small to be considered a threat. As though the worry they felt was silly, unreasonable. But Shrinking destroyed families. Sometimes love didn't grow back, especially when the shrinker gave up more than half of what they had.

Aimee glanced around the narrow street, filled with people who bore the marks of Shrinking. White bandages taped just below a bit of peach fuzz where the hair had been shaved for the needle, hollow eyes and staggered gaits.

On the other side of the street, a woman refused to hold her crying child's hand. Ahead of Aimee was the grocery, run now only by a woman after her husband had Shrank too much and left her with little more than a shrug. Aimee shivered in the crisp April air. She'd wished John had come with her, but he had a client to visit.

The line for transport into the other districts was predictably long, snaking down the sidewalk and around the corner with people waiting approval to leave the Pre-Modern borders. The whole neighborhood teemed with people, but the transport station was always the worst. There never seemed to be enough officials to make the line move at anything other than a snail's pace, and those waiting beyond the tall glass doors were often short-tempered and doing anything other than their job.

Aimee joined the queue of people and reminded herself that she was far luckier than most of the others. With her light skin and tier-one transport pass, she was likely to be mistaken for a visiting social worker or other public servant rather than an actual resident and would receive priority treatment once she made it inside.

The line shuffled a few feet forward. Somewhere behind her, someone was trying unsuccessfully to sob quietly. With a jolt, Aimee realized most of the people around her were probably on their way to see a Shrink, too. She wondered for a moment why someone hadn't opened an office here, in the Pre-Modern, but obviously, she realized, it was because no one here could afford their primary service.

As the line moved a couple of steps, Aimee stole a look around her. Mrs. Washington, the elderly woman who lived up the block, was standing only a few people in front of her.

Behind her were more neighbors, none whose names had stuck, but Aimee recognized many faces. The man behind her nodded his head and raised an eyebrow. Aimee twisted around and took a few quick steps to catch up with the line that had left her behind.

"Aimee, dear." Mrs. Washington's floral skirt swished around her ankles as she gave up her spot and instead took the one directly in front of Aimee. "How are you?"

"Oh, I'm fine," Aimee said after a long breath. "How are you?"

"Fine, fine." Aimee's eyes flicked up. Mrs. Washington's hair was covered in a scarf that matched her skirt. "Just off to the Shrink's. Had a new grand-baby a month ago, a little off the top should help with the bills." She took a few steps backward, as though she could sense that the line had moved.

Aimee's brow furrowed. "I can't believe they raised

the taxes again."

"Every few months, something goes up," Mrs. Washington said with a sage nod. "It's expensive to be poor. What about you? Off to see family?"

Family.

Aimee hadn't actually seen her family almost since she'd started "slumming it," as they'd called it. No one had been supportive of the move, and they had told Aimee she was welcome home as soon as she'd gotten this phase out of her system.

"No," she said with a smile. "I'm actually on my way to see the Shrinks myself."

Mrs. Washington raised an eyebrow and stared at Aimee.

"We had a few unexpected expenses, and then there's the taxes..." Aimee felt the heat rising to her cheeks.

"Mmmmmmm," Mrs. Washington said. "Thought you had a big savings account and a good job?"

"I did, and I do, but like you said, being poor is expensive." Aimee tried for a small smile, but it felt closer to a grimace.

"Mmmmmmm," was all Mrs. Washington said.

As Aimee had predicted, things went much faster once she made it within the gray walls of the transport station. A security guard waved her past the small cubicles where Mrs. Jefferson and others who had entered before Aimee were being questioned, and onto the smaller line of people waiting for actual transport. A large man with russet skin was trying to negotiate with the operator, pointing from the four-person transport to his five children to the sign reminding travelers that minors could not travel alone.

Shrinking had caused an uptick in single parents, and it was always a game of chance on whether an attendant would look the other way or stick to the rules. Aimee had seen this argument play out many times since she'd moved out here, and she could tell by the way the attendant stood that he wasn't going to back down.

Aimee rolled her eyes and picked at her nails. She wished she had polish on them, but color would draw attention and she didn't want John to know she was visiting the manicurist. It was her secret splurge.

"Next set!" the attendant called as he gestured to the transport tube. Aimee didn't need to look to know the man and his children were heading back to their home, wherever that was.

Aimee climbed into the tube behind a man and a woman who looked to be a couple, and a third woman who smiled into the screen embedded on her wrist. Aimee craned her neck to get a better look. "Is that a third gen?" she asked the woman.

"It is. The screen is so clear! And the calls are too!" The woman brushed her blond hair from her shoulders with her other hand and held her wrist out to Aimee. "It's amazing."

Aimee bent close and gave the woman a tight smile.

She moved her wrist closer to her side, hiding the second gen she was still wearing. Once, Aimee had had all the new gadgets when they came out. Not since she and John had moved though. It wouldn't be much longer, she told herself, until she and John got on track again, and she could buy the newest toys whenever she wanted.

Crossing into the Modern was like entering an alien world. Unlike the unique homes in the Pre-Modern area, everything was polished and uniform. Nothing was ramshackle, no building was garishly painted, nor was there litter on the ground. Here, the buildings were sleek and gun-metal gray. Everything was orderly and designed to be pleasing.

Aimee gave a little sigh of yearning as she stepped onto the familiar streets, opting to stand while the sidewalks moved on her behalf. She glanced around at all the happy faces: stylish women and dapper men, catalog-ready children. No one here showed signs of Shrinking. A frown crept into the corners of her mouth. This was where she and John belonged.

The nearest Shrink's office was only a few blocks from the transport station, nestled among various shops and restaurants. Its tall windows were opaque from the outside, but within, Aimee knew they would appear clear and full of the day's sunlight. She paused a few feet from the door, closed her eyes, and conjured John's face, his hands, his laugh. When she left this place, she would love him twenty-five percent less.

The man behind the reception desk looked up and smiled with unnaturally white teeth as Aimee walked in. He stared a little too long, and then frowned—a sure sign he had a visual implant. "Hello, Ms. Carter. I see you don't have an appointment today. Have you come to schedule one?"

Aimee worked her jaw and wrung her hands. This was harder than she expected. "No," she said slowly. "I'm here to, uh... I'm here to sell."

He stared at her again, Aimee fidgeted while he gathered more information. A slight gasp told her he'd found her address. It dug in like a knife to know he didn't think she belonged there either. "Yes, of course. Please have a seat over there." He pointed to the right, where several bedraggled people waited on flimsy chairs. Aimee joined them and looked beyond the reception desk, where clients waiting to use the office's more acceptable services waited on chairs that fit the modern aesthetic.

Aimee sat in the corner, away from the others waiting for a Shrink. On the chair next to her, a blond woman smiled up from the front of a discarded pamphlet for the clinic's services. She picked it up and flipped through to keep from being bored.

New Feeling Therapy Centers

At New Feeling, we understand that trauma large and small can make life seem unbearable. With the help of state-of-the-art extractors, our therapists can remove the feelings associated with those difficult memories while leaving your recollections of the event intact.

On the following page was a detailed explanation of the process, which assured the reader over and over that extraction did not alter memories, only the patient's feelings about the memories. Aimee shook her head and flipped to the back of the pamphlet.

Shrinking

At New Feeling Therapy Centers, we love when others share the love! Whether a happy childhood, a healthy romantic relationship, or the birth of a new child, New Feeling Therapy Centers can help you give your happy, untainted feelings to others while ensuring you still feel the joy yourself! Ask about our low-pain process and competitive rates today!

Aimee smiled. She knew all about sharing the love. It had been a monthly ritual among her social circle for years. Aimee leaned back and let the memory of her first taste wash over her.

It had started off as a girls night. Tina was going through a bad break-up and called on Lanie, Steffy, and Aimee to raise her spirits.

"'You're not enough for me...'" Tina made a sour face into her drink and shook her head. "Who says that?"

"An asshole," Steffy said sagely.

"Right, an asshole." But Aimee could tell by the way Lanie's eyes traveled over the thrumming dance floor, how they lingered on shirtless men and nearly topless women, that she wasn't really paying attention to what she was agreeing with.

"I would never say that to someone," Tina slurred, finishing her sixth drink.

"No, you just stop returning their calls." Tina had just enough awareness to glare at Steffy, but not to find an appropriately hurtful reply.

"Hey," Lanie cut in. "I thought we came out to have fun." She slapped her hands on the table and stood, her vinyl boots squeaking on the way up. Three pairs of eyes settled on her, and with a grin, she reached into the hidden pocket of her jacket. On the table she lay four small vials. Their shimmering gold liquid enough for exactly one person each. "Wanna get 'high on a feeling'?" she giggled.

Tina perked up immediately, her eyes finally becoming bright behind her many layers of makeup. "Oh! Let's do it! I've always wanted to try it!"

Aimee had shrugged and grinned. Only Steffy had been cautious.

"Isn't that stuff a little dangerous though? Don't people take advantage of Feelers?" She pulled her jacket tighter, as though someone might already be descending on their table.

"I do it all the time, and no one's taken advantage of me," Lanie laughed with a wicked grin. "At least, not in a way I didn't want them to."

"Come on, Steffy, let's live a little," Tina said before turning to Aimee. "Tell her, Aim. This is what I *need.*"

Aimee threw an arm around Steffy's shoulder. "You heard her, she *needs* this. I promise, I won't let anyone take advantage of you."

It had been, Aimee recalled, like taking a shot of warm honey. The gold liquid moved slowly down her throat and spread from her center to every corner of her body. The world took on a glow Aimee had never seen. Growing up, Aimee had wanted for nothing. The best schools, the best clothes, the best tech. Her parents had been distant but generous, and Aimee would never have considered herself to be lacking in anything. Now though, she knew she'd never before felt love, and it was incredible.

Everything was wonderful. Everyone was beautiful. The world was an amazing place. Lanie was dancing with three people on the center of the floor, Tina nearby, but clearly not a part of their circle, Steffy was curled around Aimee, lazily petting her hair.

"I love you," Steffy murmured.

"I love you, too!" Aimee squeezed her friend's arm. "And I love Lanie. And I love Tina. And I love my parents. And Mrs. Krepple from third grade. And oh god! This is amazing!"

"Excuse me." Aimee looked up from Steffy and into a pair of pale green eyes. Attached to the eyes was a man with a gentle smile. "I think you're friend is being kicked out."

Aimee looked to where the man pointed. Lanie was, it would seem, being escorted out by a security guard in a suit, Tina trailing behind them.

"Crap. Steffy, get up, we've gotta go."

The night had ended with the foursome passing out in Lanie's apartment. Perhaps it had been a tame beginning, Aimee thought, but it hadn't stayed that way. Aimee couldn't begin to count the number of one-time partners and bizarre adventures she'd had. Before John, of course.

It was almost two hours before a Shrink came for Aimee. By then, she had watched the other waiting room empty and re-fill three times. She longed to be on that side of the clinic, with the women who looked like her, the ones with high-end chips and perfectly manicured nails. Where refreshments lined one wall and entertainment the other. She would be, one day. After she and John bought a house in the modern part of the city and she was ready to erase the trauma of living in the Pre-Modern. Soon. It had to be soon.

Aimee's Shrink was Julia, though she referred to herself by the more professional title of extraction technician. Julia led Aimee into a small, darkened room. In the center sat a leather chair with a metal arm attached to the back. That arm, Aimee knew, would soon be affixed with a needle that would pull from her some of her love for John. She pulled her hair into a high bun as Julia walked behind the chair and began turning dials on a panel there.

"We should be able to shave just the underside," Julia said. Her eyes flicked to Aimee's thick hair. "You should have plenty to hide the bandage with."

Aimee nodded and slid onto the chair.

"I'm going to attach a monitor to you," Julia said as she leaned toward Aimee's temples. "This won't hurt. They're just to confirm the purity of your love."

Aimee gave a short nod and wished again John could be here. She wanted a hand to hold, a familiar voice, anything that might make the sterile room less imposing.

Julia rolled a chair in front of Aimee and sat. "Since this is your first visit, would you like me to explain the process?"

Aimee twisted her fingers and gave a small nod. The reclining chair beneath her seemed to grow, swallowing her into its depths.

"The extraction process is almost painless. What we do is take the agreed-upon amount of love, twenty-five percent in your case, and pay a fair-market value." Julia held up a small vial half-full of a swirling gold liquid. "That love is then distributed to a third party, who gets to experience the emotion for themselves."

Aimee nodded along.

"In a minute, I'm going to ask you some questions to ensure your love isn't tainted by heartbreak, resentment, fear, or anger," Julia continued, gesturing to the wires connected to Aimee's head. "This machine will monitor your responses and give me an indication for how pure your love is."

Aimee nodded again. "What about... What about right now? Does being here degrade it?"

Julia smiled and patted Aimee's hands. "Not at all. This is situational anxiety; it's not attached to the person you love, so it won't make a difference. Are you ready?"

"Okay."

"How did you meet John?"

"He saw me at a cafe," Aimee smiled at the memory. "He ran to a florist, bought a bouquet of pink roses, and got back just as I was leaving. He gave me the flowers and asked me out." Aimee held the moment behind her eyes. John, out of breath from running, holding out the trembling flowers, begging to know her better.

"Then what happened?" Julia asked.

"We went for lunch and talked for so long that we went for drinks and then dinner. A few months later I met his family—his mom is wonderful—and then a year after that we moved in together."

"Tell me about the most loving thing you've done for him."

Aimee started to gesture around the room. Moving to the Pre-Modern, coming here to Shrink, it had been a monumental act of love. Heat rushed through Aimee's body and she put her hands in her lap.

"His grandma died about a month after we moved in together," she said slowly. "She had been the center of his world. They were so close. He didn't know what to do. He didn't cry or say anything, just pretended like nothing had changed for a week." She swallowed hard, remembering the way that sweet man hadn't shed a tear, even at the funeral. "When John was little, she'd make this dumpling stew when he was sick or sad. I took a day off work and kept making the stew until I got it right and that's what we had for dinner. When he tasted it, he cried and I held him until he was done."

The words hung in the air for a moment, and when it was clear Aimee was done, Julia smiled and stepped behind her. She returned with a small slip of paper. "Ninety-seven percent. You're getting a high price for this."

Aimee's heart swelled. That meant they could catch up on the bills, and maybe even be a little ahead for next month. Aimee's smiled crumpled into a frown. Catching up on the bills, being ahead, that wasn't the same as saving. That didn't put them any closer to living in the world she belonged in. It didn't get her new clothes and toys. It didn't let her see her friends or buy manicures. It wasn't enough. She shut her eyes and rubbed her temples. The wires there were beginning to itch a little.

"Julia," she took a deep breath, "what if I gave it all?"

There was a little gasp behind her. "*All* of your love for him?"

"Yes." She smoothed her skirt and felt a weight lift from her shoulders.

"Well." Julia's voice trembled. "You'd get four times the original amount, plus a one-hundred percent bonus."

That, Aimee thought, would easily be enough to get her back to where she belonged, especially if her parents let her come home. Aimee felt a hand on her shoulder.

"Aimee," Julia said, "this is pure love. I'm looking at the results and you really love him. You know that, don't you?"

"Yes," Aimee said, twisting in her seat to face Julia. "I love him with all my heart. But I can always make more."

The Passport

by John Miller

It takes a few minutes to read.
The news should make you afraid. It would take
only a few minutes and your answer
not good enough for them in halting English

puts you in the van.
They give you no hour.
You're driven deeper and deeper into some
directionless maw of the state.

A few hours into finding out
I don't know if I could stop shaking
enough to find out if there's some way
I could make this a quickly-corrected mistake–

they would tell me it takes weeks, months,
or that when I next speak to you
it will be through the brittle copper of being nowhere,
all you ever had of this country

revealed as nothing-thinness, as paper.
So, I will take a minute now and call you,
tell you to carry your passport,
because they pick up people who look like you,

carry it a few weeks, maybe,
as if burdens of skin, language or birth
resolve by any change in status, ceremony
or oath.

Mamá,
it would take me saying it, take a minute,
carry it, that blue-and-eagle proof,
even if it has words in it they say
don't want you, take it
everywhere you go,

and you don't give it over, you don't let them take it,
you don't let them say it, not for a second, turn away,
walk away,
keep the door closed,
don't give them the first word,
not at your house, not
in your home, not in your—

Not Even Asking

the Right Question

by Christopher Mark Rose

It should be a waning crescent tonight, thirty-nine percent, rising at 2:55 a.m. Even though we can't see it now, here in the tunnels. We always know where it is. Or where it should be. For Jane and me, it's personal.

Now a figure steps towards us from the tunnel's mineral darkness, its arms outstretched, and Jane's startled yelp cuts through me. We had expected only robots.

The truth sloshes in a two-gallon bug-sprayer hung from nylon straps on my shoulder. I push it behind me, protecting it with my body. Jane unholsters the stun-gun but doesn't point it.

"Добро пожаловать! Я библиотекарь," the approaching figure says, a man, ancient in blue jeans and a down vest.

We call ourselves Seveners. Today, groups of us are descending to the strong, deep places, those likely to endure, to hide there our data and account of the objective truth, formatted to endure millennia. It will survive, far after the Deniers are gone. That's the plan, anyway.

Chernobyl. Yucca Mountain. Challenger Deep. Nuclear bunkers east and west. Gagarin Ravine on Mars. Lake Baikal. The Chevé Cave system. The Wake Shield Facility. The vestige of Antarctic ice. We'll be in all these places.

"欢迎！我是图书管理员..." says the figure.

Jane points the gun at his face, as he steps towards us.

Here we stand, Jane and I, having broken into the great seed vault at Svalbard. We are trying to do our part, to make sure the truth survives. Five ounces of plastique and a laser cutter was all it took to get in.

"Velkommen. Jeg er bibliotekar..."

I can see Jane's finger go to the trigger now, her breath held. He's maybe seven steps away.

The map we have is old. The vault has changed over a century and more, grown profound and convoluted, a vast tangle of tunnels and ramps dug deep into rock, grown haphazardly where need, funding, and geology converged.

The figure finally arrives at English. "Welcome! I am the librarian. Say your authoriz—"

"It's a hologram," Jane says, now over her earlier fright. She holsters her gun, shakes her head, and steps through the figure to the tunnel beyond. I thumb a shell and drop it; it projects holograms of two entirely different people, a couple lost and imploring. They will keep the AI that is directing the librarian occupied for the little time we need. I hope.

I think again of the Moon and our daughter Ellie. They haunt our steps tonight.

Will any of this work? Will the other Seveners teams even survive the night? We may not live to find out.

The twenty-second century is a great writhing mating-ball of slithery untruths. Computers can make any lie seem real. But the event in question wasn't something that could have been faked; not hoaxed-up from media reports, puppet-bots, 3D CGI. During those six hours and change, every person willing to step outside could witness it: the Moon glitched.

First there had been one Moon, our steadfast fellow traveler, a sober waxing crescent. Then, a second and a third appeared, seeping into being, half-moons waxing and waning on opposite sides of Earth. A little later, the waning half-moon disappeared, reappeared, disappeared, taking little peeks at us.

A full moon loomed low across the horizon, orange and raving. A silvery crescent strobed across the sky. A gibbous waning, cheese-hued, arrived then left, then came again softly. A half-moon wandered west to east, curious and peregrine, as if tacking against the sky.

They performed a slow, stuttering dance. Jane held my hand through the end, as we watched it together. An eerie cluster of feelings held us: disbelief, fascination, a trickle of fear. We looked up into the crowded sky, then down at our own feet, where faint shadows met and crossed. Seven were the most at any one time, though many more phases visited us in that six-hour period.

Astronomers assured us the event was genuine, but that was never really a question. Tides surged, weather patterns spasmed, dogs bayed. Telemetry from lunar satellites, and the voice of the astronaut at the lunar station, were hopelessly garbled.

Finally only the original remained. The Earth went on its way. But we knew in that moment that our understanding of the universe had been undermined. Six hours, thirteen minutes, and forty-nine seconds was all it took to shatter mankind's materialist philosophy, our fundamental understanding of the world.

Before that moment, materialism had won out. Science had all but proven that everything could be explained by physics. Even consciousness, but one bright bridge further, could be modeled, seemingly, on an entirely mundane but sufficiently large computer.

The Seven Moons Event made a mockery of materialist science. It wasn't even asking the right question. Physics could tell us how matter behaves—an electron, or a galaxy—but not what matter is. Metaphysics, long an embarrassing, unruly step-child, was pushed out to center stage and made to recite her part. Being qua being.

Are we stumbling down the unlikely forking of an infinite tree of universes? Are we part of some grand simulation, its operator prone to error or whim? Representations in some higher-dimensional hologram? How could we know?

Does the Moon exist?

The Moon became the most studied object in history. Robots raked and pinged every meter, looking for something, anything on which to hang a theory. That lonely astronaut wandered its surface, searching for anything that could convey a larger meaning, a sense of intent.

But those days are over now. In spite of all efforts, it remains, at least to us, an inert, uninteresting rock.

The Seven Moons Event shattered some theologies, supersized others. Churches, mosques, temples, their leaders and laypeople, all wrestled with new, unlooked-for revelation. But humanity was not ready. We couldn't accommodate revelation.

Conspiracy theories abounded. People could always lie to themselves, but they preferred when it came from an authority. Anything to shore up the crumbling status quo. A decade on, even the basic facts were in dispute.

It was madness. The President and his cronies didn't want to admit that it had happened—couldn't imagine how to even approach the issue. He started broadcasting the official orthodoxy, and public opinion became frozen in denial. He was gaslighting the planet.

It wasn't long before Seveners, those who

remembered the event faithfully, who documented it accurately, were suppressed here, and in several parts of the world. Called out in schools and churches. Accused and mocked at rallies. Fired from jobs. Forced into hiding in attics and basements. Put in jail for their beliefs.

Maybe we, too, have reacted with madness. But we had to do something. We, Jane and I, are both scientists, and so proud of our daughter. Everything we did, up to that moment, was living as an example for her. Rationalists, activists, passionate scientists—we couldn't turn aside, even if we'd wanted to.

If, in this epoch, humans are not prepared for this, then the truth must be preserved. Until.

We cannot know if the event will happen again on any timescale. But someday, there will come those who will need this evidence, and can make from it a better understanding of the world.

Now we stumble down the dark tunnel, Jane and I, with only infrared monocles and a paper map, invisible and untethered from the electronic world. We choose the most downward path, punching through an airlock, arriving at a long, dark cavern. Rows of metal shelves stand indifferently before us. We walk straight through, to the irregular rock walls beyond.

A dingy soccer ball sits abandoned, as if someone in ages past had played a game between and under the shelves. Jane touches it with a toe, and it rolls.

Nobody knows what the Seven Moons Event meant, or if it could 'mean' anything. Here's what I think it could be trying to tell us: if you have in your life one person that is singular and beautiful, someone whose presence illumines your life and makes it meaningful, then you have the capacity within you to imagine a multiplicity. If you can see a tree, then you can imagine a forest.

I think that was the last hour we were a normal family.

Ellie, her voice, coming to us through curtains of static, some distant radio dish turning infinitesimally. We—patched in directly, hardware and cameras spread across the dining room table, and the whole world watching, listening—the weird coincidence of its timing.

We had an everyday chat, talking with our daughter about weather, schedules, the impending Thanksgiving holiday, the dreary freeze-dried dinner Ellie had eaten, the pie Jane had put in the oven just before.

Then a second Ellie spoke. She introduced herself, uttered the callsign, followed the protocol the other Ellie had used a moment before.

At first we thought it was some trick of radio waves and atmospheres, a long reflection, her voice bouncing off clouds. It was her, surely. You recognize the voice of your own child. The news cameras were still running. We smiled, had the same conversation a second time. A mundane little talk.

Then the third Ellie interrupted the second. "Who is this?" she said. "Who's using this frequency?"

I knew then something was wrong. The Ellies started to argue. Jane's voice caught, and then she stopped speaking, stopped trying to make sense of a seemingly unreal event. Tears streamed down her uncomprehending face. I looked for news reports, those 'breaking news' chyrons. Then I looked up, out the window, and I saw it.

It was beautiful and uncanny, real as a fairy tale. Something that had never been seen before—or even imagined—not with this Earth, anyhow. And I knew then, that there would be more voices, a great conversation in the sky.

You see, Ellie was that astronaut. She was on the Moon when it happened. Because of some crossover in re-crewing and resupply missions, she had been the only one there.

The cameras were remorseless. They continued recording as understanding rolled over us, and we tried to respond to them all, our sudden daughters, to tell them what we could plainly see. To convince the Ellies. They laughed, unsure, unbelieving.

Eventually, some NASA administrator somewhere cut the line. Our conversation went dead. The pie had burned. We went outside and stood bathed on all sides by moonlight and amazement.

I failed to find any words to share, that first day after the Event, and the next, and the next. Silent as the Moon. What was there to say? I thought I'd lost Jane. The whole world around her had stopped making sense.

Now, in this twilit tunnel, I feel her put her hand on my shoulder. Jane, my fierce wise beautiful astronomer. It took us years to climb back to sense, and some kind of equanimity with life, after that moment. People will convince themselves, time and time again, that the things that they can't comprehend simply didn't happen. But Jane never gave up on looking up at the night sky and wondering.

I turn to look at her face, gibbous here in the dark, and she smiles ruefully.

Jane couldn't be talked out of coming to Svalbard. I really tried. She wanted to do this as much as anybody; there was no doubt in her. She would do it, whatever the price.

Listen to me now: stand in the light of the whole truth and nothing else. Don't ever capitulate to a lie, especially one that erases people, their experiences.

Ellie's testimony was purged from the records, her radio transcripts somehow buried under a classification system imposed by politicians desperate for a calming silence. Officially, NASA is keeping her there under some policy of 'quantum quarantine.' None of it is rational. After the initial efforts to understand what had happened, they pulled everybody else home. Less and less money has gone to NASA's lunar efforts. Now they barely send her supplies.

We wrote letters. We made signs. We protested out in front of the White House. We were arrested again and again, roughed up by cops. We slept in jails while waiting for lawyers' calls. What else would parents do?

Jane made an impassioned speech before a Senate committee. When I looked up, half the eyes in the room were brimming with tears. But no reporters or cameras were allowed in that closed hearing.

Then she said, "I can see my talking here wasn't worth the spit it cost me," and she spat on the senatorial podium. "All I want is my child back!"

That's when they hauled us out of there. I'm sorry for the guards I might have hurt, but I'm not sorry for anything she said—I never did get a chance to say my own piece.

They'll never let Ellie come home now. They won't admit that it happened, that she was there when it happened. Some of them won't even admit our daughter exists. They say that we're part of some conspiracy, some "false flag" operation. Admitting her would mean admitting that they don't really understand, well, anything.

We talked to Ellie, a while back. We have friends in West Virginia now, ham operators. They keep a big chicken wire dish up in the hills, away from prying ears. They have to keep moving it, so the Feds can't triangulate their setup.

She plays a lot of solitaire up there. Watches old movies, practices her Garbo imitation. Talks to the radio hams. She has a lot of time. She's getting good at growing lettuce, and the eggplants are coming along. She's keeping a diary. Nights, she plays a little flute she made from regolith plastic.

The Moon, reflected in the bottom of a well, is still the Moon.

Ellie knows she's not coming home now. Ellie knows we love her.

All that truth sloshing around in a two-gallon tank.

In the cavern I pump the plunger on the sprayer, pull the lever. The message shoots out, dark and inky, coating every surface of the wall ahead of me. I paint the seed vault with it, as high and far as I can reach.

No force on Earth will be able to scrub our message from these walls. They can irradiate it, lase it, mill it, mine it with nanobots—it will persist. It is written there, encoded in the material make-up of the ink, in a dozen clever ways: DNA, holographic crystals, quantum dots, photonic polymers, and more. The future will read our message, our astronomical data, our precise lunar observations. Our testament.

I want to believe that. I need to believe it. I need a future that thirsts for the truth.

I pump it again, but there's no more truth left in the

jug.

"Oh Jane," I say, and try to smile. We turn to go. Closer now, alarms are ringing, drones convening to hunt us down. Maybe we will escape, maybe not. It doesn't matter now.

If we do this today, we can begin to forgive them— the liars, the Deniers—for what was done to us. We stumble down a dark corridor, seeing just the things immediately in front of us. This is all that humanity has ever done.

The people who receive this data won't be born, possibly, for centuries, millennia; maybe much longer... if there are people then, and if they have the strength to confront the truth. For them, it will be a grand mystery to be solved.

But if we do this today, for us, it's hope.

Anthem

by Bethany Lee

(First published by Fernwood Press, May 2019)

When they burn the papers
And pull the plug
On half the truth
Always the worst half
And sit, bereft and blinking
In the sudden silence
And fear

I want to be the one who speaks
And rhymes love with love

When the weary marchers take to the streets
With no voices anymore
Hoarse from shouting at the wall
And done with the violence of rage
And the rage of violence
And they drop their fists and wonder

And wander toward the edges

I want to be the one who sings
And rhymes love with love with love

When the unimaginative have imagined the
unimaginable again
And the camps come for us
And the fences wind themselves around our bodies
And none of it worked
And everything failed
And hope was a mirage in a desert of tears
And all is lost but loss and the ashes
Of the lives that blazed in beauty and in joy
And some are beginning to remember to decide to hold
hands anyway
(And some never stopped remembering to hold hands
anyway)
And some are bearing witness while others give away
their bread

We will be the ones, with poetry in our hearts
Who rhyme love with love with love with love with love
with love with love

About the Authors

Rosanne Parry is the author of the many award winning novels including *Heart of a Shepherd*, and The Turn of the Tide (Random House), *Last of the Name* (Learner) and *A Wolf Called Wander* (HarperCollins & Andersen Press). *A Wolf Called Wander* spent 17 weeks on the New York Times bestsellers list. Rosanne and her family live in an old farmhouse in Portland, Oregon. She writes in a tree house in her back yard.

Janet Burroway is the author of plays, poetry, children's books, and eight novels including *The Buzzards, Raw Silk, Opening Nights, Cutting Stone* (all Notable Books of The New York Times Book Review), and most recently *Bridge of Sand*. Her plays have received readings and productions in Chicago, New York, London, San Francisco and Los Angeles. Her *Writing Fiction*, now in its ninth edition, is the most widely used creative writing text in America, and *Imaginative Writing* is in its fourth edition. She is author of the memoir Losing Tim (Think Piece Press, 2014). Winner of the 2014 Lifetime Achievement Award in Writing from the Florida Humanities Council, she is Robert O. Lawton Distinguished Professor Emerita at the Florida State University.

Carolyn Adams, originally from Houston, TX has lived in Beaverton, OR since 2017. She received her undergrad degree in Humanities from the University of Houston in 2016. From childhood, her passion has been reading and writing poetry, and she discovered collage art about 20 years ago. Her poetry, photography and collage art have been published in journals such as *Wend Poetry, Cascadia Rising Review, Steam Ticket, Caveat Lector, VoiceCatcher, Common Ground Review, Hawaii Pacific Review, Willawaw Journal,* and *Visitant,* as well as anthologies such as *Enchantment of the Ordinary* (Mutabilis Press), and *Shout* (Not A Pipe Publishing), among others. She has authored four chapbooks, has been nominated for a Pushcart prize, as well as for Best of the Net, and was a finalist for 2013 Houston Poet Laureate. She is currently a staff editor for Mojave River Review, and is on the Executive Board of the Oregon Poetry Association.

Benjamin Gorman is the author of *The Sum of Our Gods, Corporate High School, The Digital Storm: A Science Fiction Reimagining of William Shakespeare's The Tempest,* and *Don't Read This Book. Corporate High School* became an Amazon bestseller in 2016, and *The Digital Storm* was named a "Top Five Book Pick" by the San Diego Union Tribune. Benjamin is a high school English teacher. He lives in Independence, Oregon with his son, Noah. Benjamin believes in human beings and the power of

their stories. He places his confidence in his students and the world they will choose to create if given the chance.

Lydia K. Valentine is a writer, editor, educator, and dramaturg. Lydia seeks to amplify the voices of those who are often stifled, ignored, and marginalized in what has been the accepted narrative of the United States through her own writing and the projects to which she contributes. A two-time Tacoma Poet Laureate runner-up, Lydia is looking forward to the publication of her poetry collection, *Speak Me Into Being*, and staging of her play *Aliquippa*.

Zack Dye is or has been an attorney, author/poet, bar owner, tax accountant, international business liaison, teacher, researcher, traveler, soccer coach and editor. He is a restless mind and soul who hopes to someday figure out what the hell he's doing on this planet. He has a bachelor's degree in economics and American studies from Tufts University, where he took a special interest in English literature and minority studies. Since then he has worked

in Europe and South America before being admitted to the New York State Bar. He is close with his family and friends, trying to be a good son, uncle, dogfather and, in general, confidant to others who are equally confused about what this planet Earth is about.

Rebecca Smolen is a writer based in Portland, OR transplanted from NH in 2014, she has a deep love for short story, poetry, snuggling and animals. She grew up on a dead-end road exploring drainage pipes and pond life. She has a strong feminist voice that sometimes gets trapped within society's confines, but vows to teach her son and daughter to break through those boundaries Rebecca is certified to lead writing classes in the Gateless Method. Her chapbook, *Womanhood and Other Scars* is available now from The Poetry Box. You can find her writing most recently in the *Unchaste Anthology*, Vol. 2 & 3, *Mutha Magazine*, *VoiceCatcher*, and forthcoming in *Poeming Pigeon-Cosmos*.

Eric Witchey has made a living as a freelance writer and communication consultant for over 25 years. In addition to producing many corporate non-fiction titles, he has sold more than 150 short stories and several novels. His stories have appeared in ten genres and on five continents. He has received recognition from New Century Writers, Writers of the Future, Writer's Digest, The Eric Hoffer Prose Award program, Short Story America, The Irish Aeon Awards, and other organizations. His  How-To articles have appeared in *The Writer Magazine*, *Writer's Digest Magazine*, and other print and online magazines. When not teaching or writing, he spends his time fly fishing or restoring antique, model locomotives.

Heather S. Ransom has served as a middle school science and careers teacher for twenty-seven years, allowing Heather an intimate look into the minds of thousands of young adults, most of whom are desperate to find their place in a society constantly changing around them. Many have found escape, ideas for facing challenges, or simply hope for a future where they can make a difference, through reading. So every year, even though she's teaching science, Heather has her classes read. And they imagine together what their futures might hold, telling stories about advances in technology that could change their world. Her novels *Going Green* and *Greener* are available now, and the final instalment in the trilogy, *Back to Green*, will be released this year.

Joanna Michal Hoyt lives with her family on a Catholic Worker farm in rural upstate New York where she tends goats, gardens, guests and neighbors during the day. In the evening she reads and writes odd stories. The stories she loves most bring her compassionately inside the minds and lives of people who are very different, celebrate the

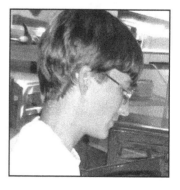

wonder that fills the world, and give her a fresh perspective on the thorny issues she wrestles with during the day. Her experiences farming in an increasingly unstable climate and working intermittently with immigrants and refugees inform her story "In the Days of El Dorado." More of her previously published short stories can be seen online at https://joannamichalhoyt.com/

Stephen Scott Whitaker is a member of the National Book Critics Circle and the managing editor for *The Broadkill Review*. Whitaker is a teaching artist with the Virginia Commission for the Arts, an educator, and a grant writer. His poems have appeared in *Oxford Poetry*, *The Scores*, *Grub Street*, and *Anderbo*, among other journals. He is the author of four chapbooks of poetry and a broadside from Broadsided Press. *Mulch*, his novel of weird fiction is forthcoming from Montag Press in 2020.

Karen Eisenbrey lives in Seattle, WA, where she leads a quiet, orderly life and invents stories to make up for it. Although she intended to be a writer from an early age, until her mid-30s she had nothing to say. A bit of free time and a vivid dream about a wizard changed all that. Karen writes fantasy and science fiction novels, short fiction, and the occasional poem if it insists. She also sings in a church choir, plays drums and sings backup in a garage band, and found herself writing songs for her debut YA novel *The Gospel According to St. Rage* (Pankhearst, 2016, Not a Pipe Publishing, 2019). She's also the author of *Daughter of Magic*, *Wizard Girl*, and *Barbara and the Rage Brigade*. She blogs (mostly about band names selected from local nightlife listings) at https://kareneisenbreywriter.com/blog/ She shares her life with her husband, two young adult sons, and two mature adult cats.

Meagan Johanson is native to Corvallis, Oregon, where she still lives with her husband and two children. She writes personal essays, poetry, and fiction, short and long. She holds degrees in English and German from Portland State University, as well as a MAT from Pacific University. When not writing, she is either reading, submersed in music, gaming, or making someone a grilled cheese sandwich. She loves a good fantasy, and believes dragons, like headphones, will never go out of style. She was running into walls while reading things before it was cool. A day without writing makes her twitch. She belongs to no one but herself.

TJ Berg is a molecular and cellular biologist working and writing in Sweden. She is a graduate of the Odyssey Writing Workshop. Her short fiction has appeared in *Talebones* (for which it received an honorable mention in

The Year's Best Fantasy and Horror), *Tales of the Unanticipated*, *Electric Velocipede, Daily Science Fiction, Caledonia Dreamin', Sensorama, Thirty Years of Rain,Tales to Terrify, New Myths,* and *Diabolical Plots*. When not writing or doing science, she can be found stravaigin the world, cooking, or hiking. She can be found on the web at www.infinity-press.com.

Jennifer Lee Rossman is a queer, autistic, and disabled science fiction writer from Binghamton, New York. She writes stories that her grandmother calls "interesting," with the hopes of giving marginalized people heroes they can identify with (and if it pisses off some angry old white guys in the process, all the better). Jennifer has been featured in several anthologies (two of which, Love & Bubbles and Space Opera Libretti, she co-edited). Her novel *Jack Jetstark's Intergalactic Freakshow* and her novella *Anachronism* are now available in paperback and digital. She tweets at @JenLRossman and blogs at http://jenniferleerossman.blogspot.com

Carlton Herzog resides in Hamilton, N.J. He served in the USAF as a flight dispatcher. He graduated *magna cum laude* from Rutgers University; he also graduated from Rutgers Law School where he served as Articles Editor of the Law Review. He currently works for the USPS. He paints, sculpts and writes in his spare time.

Austin Case received a Master's Degree from the University of Amsterdam in Western Esotericism and Mysticism. His academic knowledge of the occult and other peripheral phenomena has given him a unique take on fantasy and other speculative fiction. His novel *WILD, DARK TIMES* is available now. You can find him online at https://austinesoteric.wixsite.com/website or follow him on Twitter @esoteric_austin and Facebook.

Allan T. Price has a bachelor degree in anthropology and linguistics. Besides studying and writing, he has been a circus roustabout, a traffic surveyor, childcare worker and worked for the Department of Defense. Pursuing his interest in people and ideas, he has written many short stories, of which five have been published. He has also completed half a dozen novels, currently unpublished. He enjoys discussing strange ideas and watching Babylon 5, Game of Thrones, Dr Who and The Orville. He can be contact via the Allan Price – Author Facebook group.

K.A. Miltimore lives in the Pacific Northwest and writes paranormal fantasy & cozy mysteries in the wee hours of the morning. She loves mid-century fashion, 80s music and nachos (not necessarily in that order). With her husband and son, she loves exploring quirky local towns, including Enumclaw, WA (the setting of

her *Gingerbread Hag* series). Perhaps she will succeed in dragging her family to Iceland for a tour someday. She fancies herself a crafty person, both in projects and devilish schemes. In addition to a love of writing, she has a Masters in Labor & Employment Law that she is still paying off, a fondness for great Washington red wines, and re-watching the movies that she has forgotten over the years. https://www.kamiltimore.com/

Jill Hohnstein (she/her) has been writing since she was six years old when she penned her first play in which the main character, a young woman, was named Lucifer because Jill thought (still thinks) it was a lovely name. Her mother disagreed. Jill's byline has appeared in more than one ag newspaper, and, consequently, she is now a vegetarian. She lives in Salem, Ore., with a small dog and a medium-sized dog that is supposed to be a small dog, who are totally the bosses of her. Once upon a time, she decided to interview some of her friends. If you're interested in that at all, you can find their stories here: https://medium.com/@jillhohnstein

Kurt Newton has been writing poetry for most his adult life, some even earlier. His poem "Koala Bear Underwear" in the fifth grade was a big hit among classmates. His interest in politics goes way back to before he was born. His mother was a volunteer on the campaign to elect John F. Kennedy. Kurt's more recent political commentaries can be found in *More Alternative Truths, Alternative Truths: Endgame* and at *Eye to the Telescope*. His writing life (among other things) is on display at

Facebook. Send him a friend request; he could use it.

Taliyah St. James is a journalist-turned-author who writes depressing science fiction and less depressing fantasy. Her short story, Shrinking, was awarded an honorable mention in the L Ron Hubbard's Writers of the Future Contest. She lives in Albuquerque, NM, where she spends most of her time writing or playing board games. Taliyah can be found on Twitter (@taliyahstjames) and Facebook.

John Miller is founder of Portland Ars Poetica, an ongoing literary poetry workshop in Portland, Oregon open to poets who seek to hone their craft and their poems toward publication. His short fiction has appeared in *Tethered by Letters*. His poetry has appeared in *River Heron Review*, catheXis northwest press, *The Esthetic Apostle*, in the 9Bridges anthology *Over*

Land and Rising, and in *Glass Facets of Poetry*. John was born and raised in Brooklyn, New York. He has a degree in English from Amherst College.

Christopher Mark Rose is a husband and father, an electrical engineer for NASA spacecraft, and in his spare time, a writer of speculative fictions. He won the Baltimore Science Fiction Society's Amateur Writing Contest in 2015, and is a founder for the Charm City Spec reading series in Baltimore. He atteneded Viable Paradise 23, and has a scruffy first draft of a novel. He can be found on Twitter as @CChrisrose, and on Facebook as Christopher M. Rose. He keeps an infrequent blog at curiousful.wordpress.com. Charm City Spec can be found on Twitter as @CharmCitySpec, and as on Facebook likewise: @CharmCitySpec.

Bethany Lee lives and writes in Oregon's beautiful Willamette Valley and draws inspiration from her work as a hospice harpist and choral accompanist and from a life filled with the practice of paying attention. Her poetry collection, *The Breath Between*, was released from Fernwood Press in May 2019. Her latest work in progress is a memoir of the sabbatical year her family spent at sea. You

can look for it and her second book of poetry, *Etude for Belonging*, late in 2020. She manages all this thanks to a consistently casual attitude toward housekeeping and her extraordinarily supportive partner, Bryan.

Special Thanks

Zack and Benjamin want to recognize the thousands of people who are standing up and speaking out against the rising tide of fascism in the United States and around the world. We're grateful for organizations like the American Civil Liberties Union, Black Lives Matter, Planned Parenthood, and Raices: Texas. A portion of the proceeds of every copy of this book will be donated to those organizations to assist in the vital work they are doing, so thank you, Dear Reader, for supporting them with your purchase.

We also want to thank all the writers and poets who submitted to this anthology but couldn't be included because of space limits. We asked the writers if we could include their names here, and many were willing to be included to create a record that they used their gifts and bravery to stand and be counted. Our heartfelt thanks to Edward Ahern, Dana Alyce-Schwarz, Nan C Ballard, Zoe Brook, Glenn A. Bruce, Phillip Gregg Chamberlain, Dave D'Alessio, Sarina Dorie, H. A. Eugene, Geoffrey Hart, Blake Jessop, Raymond Lane, Franklin Murdock, Katana Redbird, Sharon Solwitz, Chris Sumberg, Hillary Tiefer, James Toeken, Dawn Vogel, Tonya Walter, Cristina Luisa

White, Rich Wingerter, Austin Worley, Xauri'EL Zwaan, and all the other authors who submitted. We are grateful to have the chance to stand shoulder-to-shoulder with such wonderful artists, and we hope History will remember we did our best to be the ones

"Who rhyme love with love with love with love with love with love with love"

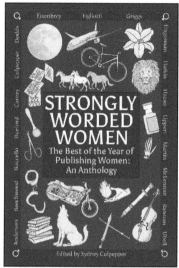

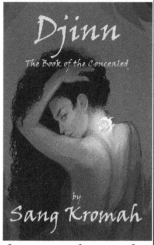

9 781948 120456